CANNING AND PRESERVING COOKBOOK FOR BEGINNERS

Preserve Your Food with Easy Mouthwatering Water Bath Canning Recipes that Save You Money and Stock Your Pantry with Healthy Delicious Food

Katie Violet

© **Copyright 2022 - All rights reserved.**
The content contained within this book may not be reproduced, duplicated or transmitted without direct written permission from the author or the publisher.
Under no circumstances will any blame or legal responsibility be held against the publisher, or author, for any damages, reparation, or monetary loss due to the information contained within this book. Either directly or indirectly.

Legal Notice:
This book is copyright protected. This book is only for personal use. You cannot amend, distribute, sell, use, quote or paraphrase any part, or the content within this book, without the consent of the author or publisher.

Disclaimer Notice:
Please note the information contained within this document is for educational and entertainment purposes only. All effort has been executed to present accurate, up to date, and reliable, complete information. No warranties of any kind are declared or implied. Readers acknowledge that the author is not engaging in the rendering of legal, financial, medical or professional advice. The content within this book has been derived from various sources. Please consult a licensed professional before attempting any techniques outlined in this book. By reading this document, the reader agrees that under no circumstances is the author responsible for any losses, direct or indirect, which are incurred as a result of the use of information contained within this document, including, but not limited to, errors, omissions, or inaccuracies.

Table of Contents

INTRODUCTION **9**
HOW IS CANNING DIFFERENT FROM PRESERVING? **12**
    Canning vs. Preserving 12
    Canning. 13
    Preserving. 13
    Preserving Food 13
    Canning Food 16
    Benefits of Canning and Preserving 21
    Canning a Boiling Water Canner 24
    Using a Pressure Canner 26
    Using a Steam Canner 27
WATER BATH CANNING **29**
    Canning Equipment 31
    Water Bath Canning Method 32
    Steps in Water Bath Canning Method 32
    Benefits of Water Bath Canning 33
    Benefits to the Home 34
    Sterilization 34
    Wide-Mouth Half-Gall on Jar 35
    Water Bath Canning Tips 36
VEGETARIAN **45**
    Chunky Zucchini Pickles 45
    Sweet Pickle Sticks 47
    Pickled Beets 48
    Watermelon Pickles 49
    Tomato Marmalade 50
    Tomato Juice 51

Green Tomato Salsa 52

Tomato Chutney 54

Tomato Ketchup 56

Dialled Green Tomatoes 58

Pickled Green Beans 59

Peppers & Tomato Salsa 60

Garlic Diall Pickles 61

Chipotle BBQ Sauce 62

Zucchini Marmalade 64

Carrot Marmalade 65

Mustard Pickled Vegetables 66

Spicy Green Tomato Chutney 68

Giardiniera 70

Spicy Carrots 72

Cabbage with Beans 73

Pressure Canned Potatoes 75

Pressure Canned Carrots 76

Celery Soup 77

Carrot Soup 78

FRUITS **79**

Peach Salsa 79

Peach Tomato Salsa 80

Apple & Tomatillo Salsa 81

Grape Jelly 82

Strawberry and Cream Quinoa Porridge 83

Mango Pineapple Salsa 84

Pear Caramel Sauce 85

Sweet & Spicy Pear Salsa 86

Chocolate Sauce 87
Mango Salsa 88
Cherry BBQ Sauce 89
Easy Peach Salsa 90
Fruit Chutney 91
Curried Apple Chutney 92
Cantaloupe Chutney 93
Orange Marmalade 95
Mango Chutney 96
Orange Cranberry Chutney 97
Cherry Rhubarb Jelly 98
Jalapeno Blackberry Jelly 99
Lemon & Wine Jelly 100
Plum Jelly 101
Preserved Fig 102

MEAT 103
Ground Turkey Taco Salad 103
Pot Roast 104
Beef Stroganoff 105
Canning Beef 106
Chipotle Beef 107
Canned Goulash 108
Canned Chicken & Gravy 109
Canned Pork 110
Chicken Stock 111
Chicken Taco Meat for Pressure Canning 112
Burrito Bowl in a Jar 113
Chopped Beef, Pork, Lamb or Sausage 114

Canned Chile, Corn & Chicken Chowder 115
Pozole Verde 116
Chicken Pressure Canner 117
Canned Chicken and Gravy 118
Chicken and Mushroom Cacciatore 119
Turkey and Green Beans 120
Canned Turkey 121
Pressure Canned Rosemary Chicken 122
Beef Bell Pepper Soup 123
Canned Chili Con Carne 124
Canned Beef Broth 125
Pressure Canned Chicken Broth 126
Chicken Tortilla Soup 127

FISH AND SEAFOOD 128

Pressure Canned Shrimp 128
Smoked Salmon 129
Pressure Canned Salmon 131
Soy Marinated Salmon Jerky 132
Ginger Miso Salmon Salad 133
Pressure Canned Tuna 134
Canned Tuna 135
Fish Chowder 136
Strong Fish Stock 137
Canned Salmon 139
Fatty Fish 141
Tuna Fish 142
Pressure Canned Whole Clams 143
Pressure Canned Minced Clams 144

Pressure Canned Shrimp 145
Canned Oysters 146
River Fish 147
Shad 148
Easy Tomato Crab Soup 149
Gina's Crab Stuffed Chicken Breast 150
Hot Crabmeat Dip 151
Janet's Appetizer 152
Fish Rice Casserole 153

PASTA 154

Garlic Oyster Linguini 154
Vegetable Soup 155
Lean Turkey Lasagna 156
Chicken Noodle Soup 158

JAM 159

Plum and Orange Jam 159
Kiwi Jam 161
Strawberry Jam 162
Blueberry and Lime Jam 163
Apricot Jam 164
Mango Jam 165
Blueberry Jam 166
Apple Sauce 167
Basil Strawberry Jam 168
Spiked Peach Jam with Ginger 169
Savory Peach Jam Preserve 171
Pineapple & Maraschino Cherry Jam 172
Triple Berry Spiced Jam 173

Apricot Lavender Jam 174
Balsamic Vinegar Ruby Port Jelly 176
Cayenne Tomato Jam 177
Mixed Berry Agave Jam 178
Strawberry-Rhubarb Jam 179
Nectarine-Mango Jam 181
Tomato-Basil Jam 182
Strawberry Freezer Jam 183
Raspberry Peach Jam 184
Tri-Berry Jam 185
Blueberry Vanilla Jam 186
Balsamic Tomato Jam 187

CONCLUSION **189**

INTRODUCTION

We are what we eat. America has a trend of eating vegan food, organic food and clean diets, but the most important thing that we all need to be eating is water. Yes, water! You have to drink enough of it each day to survive. Your body needs at least eight glasses of water a day for good health. It can also keep you from getting sick as often as well as promote weight loss and give you clearer skin.

Water bath canning and preserving is the best way to store fruits and vegetables. You can vacate them out on a counter, in a cool location, submerged in a large bowl of water. The most promising part is that you don't have to worry about any mold or freezer burn. You see, the water keeps at an even temperature and they will stay fresh for years to come!

When you are canning vegetables, whether it be pickles or pumpkin sauce, you are preserving the food of the season for later on. It's important to understand that not all vegetables can be canned in a water bath. This type of preservation is unique because boiling hot water is used to Seal jars which gives us a sterile environment for our product. This article will discuss how to can and preserve using this technique.

Canning is a process of preserving food by placing it in a sealed jar, then placing that jar in boiling water for a specified amount of time. This process kills off the harmful bacteria and all owes the food to be stored safely for up to one year. There are many types of canning including steam canning, where fresh foods are boiled for about 10 minutes; water bath canning where fruits and vegetables are placed in boiling water with enough added sugar syrup, vinegar or salt until they soften; and pressure canning, which uses high- pressure air to destroy bacteria present while preserving the flavor and texture.

When it comes to food preservation, water bath canning and pressure canning are two of the most common processes that people use in their kitchens. But when is it best to use one over the other? And how do you know which process will work best for your particular situation? Water bath canning and pressure canning both have pros and cons, but they each require specific equipment, so choosing between them may not be easy either.

Water bath canning is the oldest form of food preservation and was used in ancient Greece and Rome. A jar of water was placed in a large pot Filled with water to create a steady but not too hot water bath. If a jar never boiled over, there was no risk that the food would be damaged during the process. The downside to this method involves the heat generated when using such large amounts of hot water. It may take hours to finish heating that large amount of water up before Filling jars.

Pressure canning has been used by doctors, scientists and farmers ever since Karl Benz developed his first automobile engine in 1886. The application of this method was similar to that of canning. The pressure in the pot is increased, which increases the temperature within. A product can be canned in a pressure cooker much faster than water bath canning due to the increase in temperature and decrease in time needed for the process.

Although water bath canning or pressure canning should both be used for preserving food for long-term storage, there are several things that should be considered when choosing which one is right for you. For example, individual products vary greatly in consistency, composition and liquid content, making some types of foods more suitable to steam canning or pressure canning than others.

There are also different types of equipment in which water bath canning or pressure canning can be done, including a steam table, stove-top canner and a pressure cooker. If you plan to use the stove-top method for water bath canning, it is important to keep in mind that you will need a heavy-duty pot made of steel with a tight lid. It must be able to withstand temperatures that may rise as high as 240 degrees Fahrenheit. You will also need rubber gloves and your food must have been Prepare before you begin preserving it.

If you choose the pressure cooker method, it is important to understand what temperatures the appliance needs to reach. You should check your cooker's manual for specific information. Another thing to keep in mind is that the pressure cooker must be able to reach the maximum pressure dictated by the manufacturer.

If you are looking to purchase a steam canner, it is best that you read user reviews before making a decision. It should also fit with your stove top so that it can sit securely on four of its legs while another sits on a stabilizing platform or is fitted underneath the burner area. Your canning jars need to fit tightly into the rack and your food must be washed and prepare before it is put inside.

If you have a stove-top canner, you can also purchase a rack-and-ring set separately that is used to help you safely Fill your jars while they are being heated. The ring must be placed on the jar's mouth until it reaches the right height, then it needs to be removed and attached to the canner by screwing the ring half way into place. The rack is placed inside and the lid is screwed in place.

Eating healthy foods and increasing your overall health can be a challenge. Our busy lives make it difficult to always make the best choices for ourselves and our families. We want to do our best to eat nutritious food, but sometimes that is not always possible. That's why it is so essential to find ways to store foods so that they can be easily and conveniently Prepare once we get around to eating them. But although freezer bags and resealable plastic containers are good for some things, you should also consider water bath canning or pressure canning for some of your food preservation needs.

HOW IS CANNING DIFFERENT FROM PRESERVING?

Canning is the process of sterilizing mason jars Filled with a variety of fruit, vegetables, or meat and then boiling the jars to Seal m airtight. This preserves the food for much longer than just storing it in your fridge.

Preserving refers to any food that you store or keep for an extended period of time, like pickling or dehydrating produce. There is no boiling involved because this type of process kills any live bacteria in produce.
Canning and preserving are similar in that they both aim to keep food fresh for long periods of time but they differ on how they go about doing so as well as how long they will last before going bad.

Canning vs. Preserving:

For canning, food is sterilized by heat and then sealed in mason jars. After being boiled, the jars are hot to the touch but the food inside the jar is still safe for long-term storage. For example, using a boiled method for processing tomatoes will stop an existing colony of bacteria from growing on your canned tomatoes if any have been infected. This process also kills all harmful bacteria that may be present in canned foods which means it can last anywhere from several years to decades if properly stored after opening each package.
For preserving, no heat is used, so the food is not sterilized. However, since the bacteria present in produce is killed during the preserving process, you will be able to eat your preserved produce much faster than something canned. For example, a jar of jam that uses pickling methods can be eaten as soon as its opened whereas a jar of tomatoes that have been preserved for several months must sit for 24 hours before being consumed.

The difference between canning and preserving makes it important to understand what food preservation method you are using when you are storing food because each has different storage and expiration times.

Canning:

Canning is where you put food into a jar, seal it shut, and then Boil entire thing. Food that has been canned should be able to last indefinitely because the mason jars are sealed airtight. The only way for your canned food to spoil is if its not stored properly, leaving it exposed to moisture or the wrong temperature.

Preserving:

Preserving involves using water Baths, sugar syrups and salts to lower the pH or acidity of produce so that microbes such as bacteria cannot grow on them when they are dried out.

Preserving Food

Basics of Preserving: What is it and How it Works. General Step-by-step Instructions

Preserving is the process of preventing food from spoiling by using low- temperature cooking, dehydration, or refrigeration. Food preservation has been used for millennia to inhibit the growth of bacteria, yeast, and other microscopic organisms that cause spoilage. Preservatives are chemicals that prevent food from turning rancid or moldy. The development of modern methods of food storage followed surprisingly quickly in some places once Emperor Augustus of Rome created a government monopoly on wine containers in 27 BC.

There are thousands upon thousands of different kinds of preserving techniques today call ed 'methods' with many combinations to adapt to any given need on what can be preserved or how long it should last for storage purposes. Some food preservation methods simply freeze or heat a food product to destroy microorganisms that cause spoiling. Others use a combination of high-temperature techniques, such as baking, pasteurization, and irradiation. The contemporary supermarket often offers products preserved in these ways - many of which contain preservatives such as dipotassium phosphate or sodium benzoate.

The way you cook the food is just as important as what type of food is being cooked. If you over-cook the food you risk food poisoning from bacteria and viruses that may be present in the food. If you under cook the food there is a risk that it will become mushy and lose flavor and texture which can be a safety hazard for those who consume it.

The term "preservation" refers to the process of keeping food safe and usable for a period of time. Most efforts at preservation are aimed at preventing spoilage, or to extend the life of food by delaying spoilage until it can be used for other purposes.
There are three main categories of preservation: dry storage; freezing; and canning/curing. Dry storage (also known as dehydrating or respreading), disassociates water from foods, thus greatly extending their shelf life.

Freezing is achieved through the use of refrigeration and freezing to lowerthe water activity (aw) of foods, which ultimately make them safer to eat. Canning involves placing food into heated glass jars or metal cans to kiall bacteria and other microorganisms, which is especially useful for foods that aren't naturall y suited to drying (like fruit), or for producing other liquids besides water (like milk).

Most preservation techniques depend on reducing the presence of harmful microorganisms by applying heat either by using hot water or steam; hot air; or boiling food. Some preservation techniques are best suited to particular types of foods. For example, dairy products, eggs and root vegetables are preserved well through the use of fermentation. Freezing maintains the quality of frozen foods since they don't rely on just one preservation method.

Preserving is an important skill in homesteading and living off the land. The following steps will help you preserve your food and create a well- rounded pantry.

One of the first steps to preserving food is to fire up your stove. Heat a pot of water until it reaches boiling point, then drop in all sorts of squash, potatoes, carrots, and onions (or whatever vegetable you want to preserve). Once they're soft - take them out (please be careful!). You can see we've already added pumpkin puree and apple cider vinegar to this mixture.

Next we 'all Drain vegetables so they don't overcook in the saucepan. Place m in a colander and let the steam flow. We don't want to put them on top of wet paper towels or they will get soggy. Now comes the fun part - mixing! If you want chunky, traditional homemade relish, then mix the ingredients together by hand. Place in sterilized mason jars while hot, and screw on lids/rings while they're still warm.

If you want smooth relish, then you'll need to use an electric mixer or blender (or put gloves on your hands...rubber gloves work even better!). Blend until the mixture is totally smooth (this will probably take about 5-10 minutes or so). Then put the mixture into a container to cool.

If you're going to put the relish in a jar, then you'll need a lid that can withstand being heated, and it needs to be tight fitting. You can use any glass container that isn't too narrow or too tall for the jam to flow out of (in other words, make sure whatever type of jars you use are wide-mouthed and flat bottomed). You might want to wait until the mixture is at room temperature before placing it in jars. Once the mixture is in there, screw on rings or lids.

Next, heat up your pressure cooker. Once your pressure cooker reaches 10 lbs. of pressure (make sure the steam valve is closed), Reduce heat to maintain that pressure for 20 minutes (you may need to adjust the temperature depending on what type of pressure cooker you use; follow your cooker's instructions). Release any remaining pressure in a safe area away from flammable materials, then remove jars from pot and let cool completely before checking seals. If the seal isn't airtight, then the relish should be refrigerated. Unsealed jars can be placed back in your pressure cooker, unsealed side up, and relished again for 10 minutes at 10 lbs. of pressure (if you're using an All American 921 like us) or at 5 lbs. of pressure (if you're using a Presto 23-quart pressure cooker).

If you have to unseal jars for any reason before storing them in the fridge or pantry, make sure you have a clean sterile utensil to avoid contamination.

Canning Food

Basics of Canning: What is it and How it Works. General Step-by-Step Instructions

Many people start to learn about canning by reading the instructions that come with their canner. The instructions might tell them how often to use it, what ingredients they need, and what temperatures they should aim for. But there is no substitute for having a little knowledge of how canning works and what you will need in order to successfully store your food over the long term. This book will cover all of these topics and more so that anyone who wants to preserve food in jars will have a better understanding of the process and be able to enjoy safe and healthy meals from their own pantry at home without ever having to wonder if those dishes were canned safely.

The first thing you need to understand about canning is what it means to be a sealed jar. A sealed jar means that there is no air going in or out of the jar. While this seems obvious, many people overlook a simple fact: That a jar is not sealed until you put the lid on it. This doesn't mean that anything will keep your food from spoiling, just that it won't have been canned using the proper method. An easy way to remember this is to remind yourself that spoilage comes from microorganisms and oxygen, so if there's no air movement into or out of the jar then there's no way for the bacteria to spoil your food.

The next thing to know is that the seal only forms when you process the food. While non-processed jars will keep your food fresh, they aren't properly canned which means that the seal could break and air could get in, spoiling your food. The last thing you need to remember is that spoilage is not an indicator of whether or not you should eat something. You can't tell if something isn't spoiled by how it looks or smells. You also can't tell by the taste of the food. Some people even claim that they can tell when food hasn't been properly canned by tasting it, but the truth is that your senses will be fooled. There will always be bacteria in your food and they will make it look and smell bad, but not spoil it.

If you want to start canning and preserve your own food, then you need to know about pressure canning. Canning all owes you to store different types of foods without worrying about them going bad before they're ready to be eaten. When it comes to food preservation, pressure canning is one of the most talked-about methods that is used around many families today. When it comes to pressure canning, you will need a pressure canner. These come in many different sizes and shapes, but the one thing they have in common is that they all have a built-in vent at the top so that air doesn't go in and out of the canner. But this isn't the only thing you need to know about pressure canners because you also need to understand how much air it takes to process foods for pressure canning.

In order to learn how much air it takes, you first need to consider what size metal objects are inside your home when processing foods for pressure canning. If there are household items inside the canner, then the water that you are adding to it is being held under pressure. If these objects are made of metal, then you'll need to increase the amount of air that enters the canner by the amount of metal in your house. But this is where it gets complicated because different people have different things inside their homes. Some people have metal pots and pans while others have copper pipes and even some people have aluminum or stainless steel kitchen sinks. The size of these metallic objects will make a big difference in how many items you need to count towards your total amount of items.

Next you need to know about how water is used when pressure canning. Just put the number of items that are in your house into the canner, then Fill it with water until it reaches exactly the weight of the items that are in there. If you don't count all of the metal objects, then your pressure canner won't be able to hold all of its contents under pressure. You don't have to do this every time you use a new batch of water, but every time you do something different with your canner, you will need to check all of these things again unless you have a digital cooking scale on hand so that you can accurately track everything down exactly.

The last thing you need to know about pressure canning is the weight of the contents in your pressure canner. This is very important because if you don't have enough water in your canner, then it won't be able to properly Seal jars and do a good job protecting them from outside air. In order to know how much water you need, simply put all of your ingredients into a pot and weigh them. Once you have this information, you will be able to determine how much water needs to go into your pressure canner and then how much air is going into that space when you process them with the jar lids on top. There are many different ways to do this, but the easiest way is to put the lid on a jar and then measure how much space there is between the top of the lid and the edge of the jar.

After you have measured that out, then you can use this information to determine how much water you need into your pressure canner at a certain time. If you use a digital cooking scale, though, it will be easy for you to keep track of all this information without having to have a separate container for keeping track of these measurements. You should also know how to properly clean your pressure canner so that it will not only look better at home but will be able to take care of all of your food items over time.

If you want to learn more about pressure canning, then you need to know how much air is needed to process foods with the jar lids on top. You will be able to learn how much air it takes, whether or not you need different sized canners, the ins and outs of how to measure all of this information accurately and more. It's very easy to learn about pressure canning once you know what it is.

If you want to learn how to can, follow these simple steps. We have included both an overview of the process, as well as detailed instruction on each step of the process. After reading through this guide, we hope you will feel confident in your home canning abilities and be able to enjoy all the benefits this hobby has to offer.

Step 1: Determine the kind of jar you need to can in.
There are different types of jars available on the market. They include: Pint or pint-sized mason jars (approx. 2-1/2 quart)
Small Ball jars (approx. 1 pint) Large Ball jars (approx. 5-1/2 quart) Other wide mouth canning jars such as: Wide Mouth Pint and Quart above and Half Pint and Half Quart above. These can be used to can all types of pickles and jams. Some people also use these for small fruits such as cherries, raspberries, etc.

Step 2: Choose fresh, high-quality produce.
You should always start with the freshest possible ingredients. Vegetables and fruits that are not at their peak will produce inferior canned results. Choose fruits and vegetables that look and smell fresh and appetizing. You want to make sure the food inside is safe to eat and ready for your enjoyment. Most fruits and vegetables can be canned using any of the methods we describe on this page, but there may be some exceptions. For example, some produce must be pressure canned using a pressure canner.

Some fruits must be peeled before canning. There are two types of peels described here. Peels which are thin-skinned, such as peaches or pears, require only washing to remove dirt and pesticides. Such soft-skinned fruit do not need to be peeled before canning if you use one of the hot pack methods described below.

The second type of peel is known as thick-skinned produce . Examples include tomatoes, peaches, apples or any other fruit that has a tough outer skin that is difficult to cut through. These must be peeled first before they are put into the jars if using the raw pack method (which results in juicy fruit).

Step 3: Prepare your jars and canning funnel.
Canning Jars - Fill a large pot with a couple of inches of water and bring to a boil. Using your canning funnel, Fill each jar to about 1/2 inch from the top with food, then using a ladle, add 1/2 or 1 teaspoon of salt to each jar or as directed in the recipe. This is optional but it will help preserve your canned food. If you are working with small fruits such as raspberries, blueberries, blackberries or strawberries, you should prepare them by removing any stems and blanching for 1 minute in boiling water before Filling the jars with the hot fruit mix from step 5 below. Using a clean damp cloth, Wipe rims of the jars to remove any food particles. Place a lid on the jar and use your canning funnel to Fill each jar with boiling water to 1/4" from top of jar. You can either use a canning rack or a towel to hold the jars as they are being Filled.

Step 4: Process your jars in a boiling water bath .
Place your Filled jars into a large pot and add enough water so that there is about 2 inches of water over top of the jars. Cover pot and begin heating over high heat (bring water to boil). Once boiling (at sea level), set timer for 10 minutes. During this time, the jars should be covered with at least one inch of water. After 10 minutes, Remove lid and use a jar lifter to lift the jars from the pot and Place m on a towel or canning rack. Let cool completely. Once jars have cooled, refrigerate them for a few weeks before eating.

Step 5: Assemble your canning supplies.
You will need to have these items on hand for canning. A funnel, canning rack, jar lifter, jar lifter tool, dishwashing soap, dishwasher tablets or liquid bleach. You will also need to have on hand sterilized jars, lids and bands. Storage jars are available at any local grocery store.

Step 6: Wash your produce, peel it and cut it .
Wash produces thoroughly under running water to remove dirt and any pesticides. All fruits and vegetables except onion should be peeled before canning. Some fruits and vegetables should be cut in half, some in quarters. Refer to the list below for guidance on which produce should be cut into how many pieces before being placed into a canning jar.

Place into clean hot jars. Pack food firmly using a spoon or your clean hands leaving 1/2 inch of headspace at the top of the jar, if using a wide mouth jar, leave 1 inch of headspace
Refer to specific recipe instructions or use these tips for correct amount of ingredients to add to each jar

Benefits of Canning and Preserving

You can actually so much more than just saving money if you Take time to do some research on how much money is saved by eating your own food. There is actually y a lot of benefits to taking the time to do this. First off, you'll be able to get good nutrition from your food without having to worry about funds or where it comes from. Next up, you'll be able to save money by taking the time to make your own healthy food. It is also an excellent way for you to get nutrition for your body every day without all the extra costs, including additives and preservatives that are required in commercial foods. You can make your own foods that don't require special shipping around because they're completely homemade. Many people think that making their own food will cost them more because they're just not aware of what it takes into account when you Take time to do so. The fact is that if you can get more of your own food, it will end up costing less in the long run because of the costs, amount and what it takes to get commercial food. You can also make your own homemade spicy hot sauce that is known for its spicy goodness. There is a reason why this hot sauce is so popular and there are actually y several benefits to taking the time to make it yourself. It's always great to know how others make their foods and why they do it. You'll also be able to enjoy homemade foods with your family and friends on a regular basis without worrying about anything else at all . You can Take time to make really y nice homemade foods for your family and friends as well as enjoy it too.

First off, you should always make sure that you have all the ingredients for your recipe or else it will not contain anything. You'll need access to water, containers and a pot/pan as well as any other appliance that is needed to make the food. There are also several types of foods that you can choose from when storing them in your pantry, including pickles, jams, jams, jellies and many more. Making homemade jam is definitely easier than you may think.

You can also try this recipe by lowering the heat during cooking so the temperature goes down to about 350F. You'll need to wait for it to cool down before you can pour your jam into the jars because you need it to cool down for this one!

These homemade foods are great for everyone since they're easy, cost effective and are healthy as well. You are able to have good quality food that is free from preservatives or anything else that may be unnecessary or unwanted.

Who would have thought that the idea of going back to enjoying foods that we had access to before would result in a new approach to our lifestyles? This is what you get if you decide to learn how to use a glass jar for food preservation. You can go back to a simplicity that will work better for you and your family without all of the complications and costs associated with commercial food.

This means more money saved for your family because of all the savings from buying less food! Homemade canned foods are not only great tasting but they can also be healthy.

There are several things that you will need to know when you decide to make homemade canned foods. For instance, if you decide to make homemade canned foods, you'll need special equipment for this purpose. You'll need a pressure canner or an ordinary pot with a lid for this process. You'll also need jars and lids. There are several types of food that you can choose from when making homemade canned foods, including homemade canned fruit, jams and jellies and many more.

If you decide to can your own fruits that are in season, they will be the freshest produce that you could enjoy that is great for making smoothies or drinking juice. You should always make sure that you follow the instructions to the letter so you get the best results.

There are several reasons why people prefer to use glass jars for storing food. These containers are clear, which means that you'll be able to see what's inside them. Some plastic containers cannot do this because they're too dark to allow this view.

Another benefit of glass jars is that they're reusable, unlike plastic containers that are one-time use only, especially if it has BPA in it. There are also some glass jars with seals on them, which would not let oxygen in or out of the jar. It would stay in and remain there until you open it.

You may not know what the procedure is when you're making homemade canned foods. However, there are several steps to follow when you're making homemade canned foods. You should start out by washing your hands and jars well with warm water and soap. You should also prepare all of your food items before starting out on your canning session, including washing them well and cutting off the ends of the fruit correctly.

It's also important to make sure that your lids are also boiled for 10 minutes in order for them to seal properly just like a can because a jar doesn't have a bottom to it like a can does. The only way you can make sure of this is by using a rack with some jars.

When you're making homemade canned foods, you should carefully follow the instructions that are given on the can or jar packaging. You will also need to prepare your jars or lids with the right mixtures of water, vinegar and spices. Once you're done with these things, it would be easier for you to start out once everything is ready. You should also ensure that everything's completely cleaned before starting your session.

When you decide to go back to enjoying homemade food, it 'all all ow for more time spent at home with family and friends without all of the commitments associated with commercial food. This mean you will get to enjoy time with your loved ones and still get to enjoy the foods that you had access to before using glass jars.
If you haven't tried it yet, it's definitely worth giving homemade food a try!

Keeping your food fresh is easier than ever with Mason jar canning.

You'll be able to preserve all of the food items that are in season so you'll get to eat them whenever you want. There are several types of foods that you can choose from when preserving them in glass jars, including jams, jellies, pickles and more. You can also try these recipes on one of the glass jars that you have either.

There are several reasons why some people go back to using glass jars for food preservation, including the fact that they make use of them again and again without experiencing any kind of contamination. These containers also all ow you to preserve your food with ease, as well as it all owes you to enjoy the same foods that you had access to before without worrying about anything else at all .

All kinds of foods can be preserved in a jar if you're interested in learning how. You can preserve foods in a jar by preparing the jars first. You'll need to ensure that every jar has been thoroughly washed before you start out with your preservation session since you won't be able to properly preserve your food if they aren't clean. Jars should also be sterilized before you start making your preserved food so it 'all have a longer shelf life.

Canning a Boiling Water Canner

An important part of preserving food and/or your own life is canning. Canning has been used for thousands of years and is still a popular method to preserve food, especially since it kills all of the microbes that may have grown on the food.

A boiling water canner is an appliance that works by heating jars with boiling water in order to Seal m, preventing microorganisms from growing inside the jar.

Boiling water canners work in a variety of ways. Newer canners are electric while older ones are run on a stove. They all have some type of rack that holds the jars during the heating process.

When using a boiling water canner, you'll need to poke holes into the lids of your jars and Place m on the racks inside the canner.

This all owes for more water to get into the jars and for the heat to more efficiently penetrate them. The temperature is set over boiling water and once it reaches this temperature, it begins processing your food in 10 minutes or less.

Once the processing is done, immediately remove from the heat and place into your jars. Remove your lids from the canner and Seal m up to keep your food safe.

You may find that you have to replace some of your jars once you're a few years into using the canner. If you find that this is happening, then it may be time to purchase a new one or try another brand of canner.

They are available in different capacities as well as with or without water level indicators on top. You should consider how large your family is as well as how much food you plan to preserve over time before purchasing.

Once your canning is done, you'll have a variety of food to feed yourself and your family for years to come. You may even decide that you're going to start sealing it and make a little extra money on the side.

You can use boiling water canners for more than just canning, however. Some people choose to use them for cooking purposes, especially if they have older children and don't wish to stand over a hot stove while they cook dinner.

Boiling water canners are also great for making soups, boiled eggs, and even pasta and it can reduce your time in the kitchen while preparing meals. It is simply a matter of finding out what works best for you and adjusting accordingly.

If you're interested in preserving your own food or making it easier to cook dinner, don't hesitate to purchase a boiling water canner. They make life easier on those who use them and are an excellent way to save money on expensive meals out. You may even find that you'll go through less food since it will last longer in the refrigerator or freezer since you sealed it for freshness.

Using a Pressure Canner

A pressure canner is designed to build up pressure when heated, thus raising the temperature. This is very important when processing low acid foods such as meats and veggies that do not have an acidifying agent in their recipe. This is because low acid foods can create a good environment for botulism spores to grow when not exposed to very high temperatures. Botulism spores can survive the water boiling point.

The pressure canner is ideal for low acid foods at 10 pounds, and the pressure temperature is 240°F which is sufficient to destroy the botulism spores.

There are two main types of pressure canners, and these are:
Weighted Gauge Pressure Canner

This canner has a weight that is used to control the pressure. The weight can either be a flat disk that goes up to 15 pounds or three rings of weight mounted on each other.

Once the pressure inside the canner is achieved, the weights will jiggle as a sign that the optimal temperature has been reached. This makes it very easy to monitor the canning process.

The pressure required for canning is 5 pounds; for vegetables 10 pounds and for meats 15 pounds.

Dial Gauge Pressure Canner

This has a dial that shows the pressure inside the canner. As the pressure and temperature increase inside the pressure canner, the dial rises. Depending on the model, the dial may indicate 1 pound or 5-pound increments. The advantage of a dial gauge pressure canner is the fact that you can adjust for altitude.

Pressure canning uses large pots that produce steam call ed

pressure canners. Pressure canners heat the contents to 240°C. The pressure canning method is usual y used in low acid foods.

Basic Steps in Pressure Canning Method

. In a pressure canner pour 2–3 inches of hot water, arrange Filled jars on a rack and close securely.
. Open exhaust vent and steam for 10 minutes in a high heat situation, then close exhaust vent after 10 minutes.
. Let the canner pressurize for 3–5 minutes, and start timing when the proper pressure for altitude has been reached.
. Remove from heat when processing is finished. Let the canner cool and depressurize. Pause for 2 minutes before opening the exhaust vent.
. Uncover and carefully take out jars from canners. All ow jars to cool down. Keeping it away from your touch, improper handlings may cause jar breakage.
. All ow the jars to cool completely for 12–24 hours, before seal testing. The jars should retain accurate headspace and air bubbles free to pass seal testing.
. Store your food in a clean and dry space or on shelves.

Using a Steam Canner

Steam Canner is a tool that can be used to preserve the food you grow at home year round. It heats water into steam and forces the superheated vapors through an inverted canning jar. The lid is then tightly sealed with a wire bale, which traps the heat inside and keeps oxygen from reaching the food. This process can last for hours on end, depending on how long you leave it at one time. The process is not just used to preserve vegetables and fruits but can also be used to sterilize medical instruments and even items from your kitchen.

How The Steam Canner Works?

Steam canners are typically constructed out of stainless steel, with a large vented section designed for heating water. The jars are placed within the steam canner after being Filled with the food you would like to preserve. The lid is then sealed, trapping the steam within the canner and warming it up very quickly. After that, you can leave it on its own until all of your jars are done or you can manual y Turn off heat or all ow a cooling down period. It is best to wait until the lid pops up slightly before removing the jars after you have turned off the heat.

The major benefit to using a steam canner is that it offers food a longer shelf life. The process not only kills bacteria within the jars themselves, but also removes any natural water from within the food itself. This process eliminates most spoilage, making it one of the most efficient methods of preserving foods in existence. No chemical preservatives are needed with this product and bacteria are destroyed with heat only. Steam canning is also used by doctors and other medical facilities as there are no chemicals involved in sterilizing equipment or instruments which makes it very safe on the long term.

WATER BATH CANNING

Water bath canning is a technique of preserving food in jars which is primarily used for fruits and pickles. The technique uses the boiling water from a kettle to heat up the jars Filled with the food to be canned. This process of preserving foods does not require any more pressure than an average pot on a stove, and it also does not require any added tools aside from a kettle or saucepan for boiling liquids.

At present, there are many methods that satisfy the requirements of water bath canning, such as using traditional saucepans or modern pressure cookers with special jars. In recent years, a particular type of water bath canning has been developed. The method is call ed "bunching".

Aside from the benefits of batch Cooking, the method also provides a solution to handling the process equipment and reducing labor costs. After using this kind of water bath canning, scientists from Japan and Taiwan experimented with different types of canned food (bunched can-type) that are extremely difficult to open without destroying them. As a result, foods that are unsuitable for current meat or juice preservation techniques could be preserved by sandwiching in sugar or saturated with water at around 100°C for 7–8 h.

The process of water bath canning is actually the heating system which will be utilized, and it has to be done with a few easy steps. To begin, the food must be heated up to a temperature of 92°C in a kettle or saucepan before transferring it over to a jar. After being Filled up with donned jars, sealants should be applied on every single one of them. In order for all the food to have uniform cooking, hot water must then be poured into an empty space in the jar. The amount that is required for Filling depends on the size of jar used and the food content. Afterwards, the jars need to be placed in a kettle with boiling water. Depending on the size of your kettle, you can place anywhere from one to three jars inside of it. The final step is when the contents of all jars must be boiled for 30 minutes. After 30 minutes have passed, the jars are then taken out and all owed to cool down for about 12 hours.

Once this process has been finished, your foods will then be ready for consumption. However, jar lids must still remain sealed during this time so that any bacteria that might have contaminated your food will still not be able to circulate around within it.

Some other canning techniques may require more water and a longer Cooking time to completely destroy food-borne pathogenic bacteria, including Clostridium botulinum, which is the main cause of botulism. However, the water bath canning process requires less water and a shorter cooking time because it heats up the jars in boiling water instead of steam.

As a result, lower cooking temperatures are achieved using water bath canning than with other methods for preserving food at home. In addition to this, steam pressure from many types of pressure cookers may play a part in destroying extra heat-sensitive vitamins when compared to the temperature achieved by boiling water in ordinary pots or kettles. The water bath method of canning food is considered to be a very safe process which will not significantly alter the taste and texture of food. In addition, this particular process is also considered to be much less costly than other methods of canning, such as using a pressure canner. And in many cases, it is easier to Prepare as well.

Water bath canners are generally made up of two parts: the water bath itself and the jars that will be sealed inside them. Many different types of jars are available for use in water bath canning depending on the type of food being canned and is referred to as an "accepted jar size" in terms of domestic water-bath canners.

Commercial canners sold by canning supply houses typically come with their own jars. Other canners are made by individuals and may be used to preserve various types of food, such as meats and vegetables.

Other important things to think when choosing a canner include the date when the canner was last cleaned or Filled up with water (this should be at least 6 months old if the jar is to store anything for more than 12 months with no additional water). The minimum time, or "heat up time", in which water must be boiled inside the canner before removing the jars from it.

Safety is of foremost importance when it comes to canning food. In order to make sure that you are using a safe process, it is highly recommended that you purchase a canner that has been approved by a food safety agency. Make sure to Check instructions on your canner carefully before using it and avoid using any jars with cracks or chips in them. Following these instructions will help ensure your safety when canning your food and will reduce the chances of anything harmful happening during the process.

The most common concern for this method of canning may be botulism, which is caused by a bacteria call ed C. Botulinum and may be harmful by causing muscle paralysis, including difficulty swell owing and breathing. There are several actions that you can take to ensure your safety when water bath canning food, which include:

Water in the jar will begin to boil immediately and the temperature must be maintained at 92°C for a period of time.
After this process has been completed, all ow the jars in your water bath to cool down for at least 12 hours before removing them from the pot Filled with boiling water.

The canner must be cleaned thoroughly and Filled up with fresh water before each use. The same contents should then be used throughout a six-month period if it is being used to store food for any longer than that without additional water.

Canning Equipment

Water Bath Canner: a large pot with a lid and rack, it's usually used in canning high acid foods.
Pressure Canners: usually mistaken as a pressure cooker. There are two kinds of pressure canners; the dial gauge and the weighted gauge. The dial gauge measures pressure through the dial gauge

and the weighted gauge uses weights in measuring and controlling pressure build up. It also comes with wire racks. It's used in canning low acid foods.
Canning Jars: also call ed mason jars especially manufactured for canning purposes. It comes in different sizes and jars openings; wide mouth and regular mouthed jars.
Canning Jar Lid and Rims: canning jars and rims are re-usable but lids should be brand new always.
Canning Funnels: used for easier transfer of food to the jars
Jar lifter: comes in the rounded end and rubber-coated that holds jars safely and transfers jars without falling.
Large stock pot: for blanching purposes.
Wooden spoon: for mixing.
A clock or timer: to remind you of the time.
Mixing bowls: used in combining food ingredients and used as containers while cutting and peeling.
Sharp knives: for cutting and peeling.
Chopsticks or stir stick: used to get rid of remaining air bubbles.
Strainers: used to separate liquid forms from solid parts of ingredients. **Food processor:** used especially in making jams or jellies.
Ladle and spoons: used in transferring food pieces into the jars.
Tongs: used in taking off hot pot covers or lids.
Clean towels: for wiping your hands, and cleaning dirt and mess.

Water Bath Canning Method

It is also call ed hot water canning. The water bath canning method is ideal for foods with high acid contents like fruits, and vegetables such as tomatoes. Water bath canning uses large pots call ed boiling water canners. Boiling water canners are made of aluminum or porcelain-covered steel. It has fitted lids and removable racks. Jars are immersed in water and heated at 212°C for a specific length of time.

Steps in Water Bath Canning Method

- Fill water bath canner halfway, cover then boil.

- In a separate pot, boil 4 quarts of water

- Assemble jars onto the water bath canner rack; pour additional water to cover jars.

- Cover canner and let it boil, lessen the heat and continue simmering. As the water starts to boil begin timing. Turn off heat when it reaches the preferred time. Tilt lid to let steam outflow.

- Remove jars from the canners carefully and all ow them to cool

- After cooling completely, apply seal testing before storing your food.

Benefits of Water Bath Canning

Water bath canning is a relatively new way of preserving food by submerging jars in boiling water. The method keeps the food and jar from being exposed to air, which prevents bacteria from growing or spore growth from taking place. These methods can also preserve such items as beans, pickles and jams that would otherwise need to be kept in the refrigerator. Other benefits include better flavor retention and reduction of cooking time overall for those who are choosing to use this type of preservation method.
Benefits to the Food

Many people are under the impression that water bath canning only preserves food for half a year. This is incorrect, as most foods will keep for up to a year if there aren't any signs of spoilage. The reason that most people believe this is because by following proper water bath canning procedures, they are able to preserve their food better and much longer than other methods. For example, fruits and vegetables that are water bathed tend to keep better all - around because they have been preserved better from the get-go. In addition, soups and stews created with water bath can methods will last much longer without having to be frozen or refrigerated for long periods of time.

Benefits to the Home

Water bath canning has many benefits for a home that chooses this method of preservation. For one, it is much easier to clean jars than glass jars, so there is less wear and tear on the kitchen counter. Another benefit of water bath canning is that it will greatly speed up your cooking time since you are not having to wait on a hot water bath to cool down before using them. This can help save money in the long run, since slow cooker recipes require specific times and temperatures for proper cooking times. Many people choose this as their primary method of food preservation because they are able to create more wonderful meals knowing that they will last forever without having to buy fresh food each time.
Benefits to the Lifestyle

Using water bath canning methods can help improve a person's lifestyle by all owing them to save money and eat more "natural" foods without having to store them in the refrigerator. Many foods that are preserved in this manner will keep indefinitely, as long as they are prepared properly and kept in a cool spot. This is why so many people choose this type of food preservation over others, because they know they will be able to use their cans when they need them and not have to worry about making sure that they are still good years after storing them. People who choose these methods are able to focus more on cooking delicious food that is very nutritious than having to worry about how it is stored.
Many people choose water bath canning as their primary method of food preservation because it all owes them to create meal plans and make sure that they have enough food to last throughout the year. The fact that these foods will keep indefinitely in a cool, dry place makes them perfect for many homes that have limited space for storing items in a freezer or refrigerator.

Sterilization

Picking out the right jars for your canning is very important because all jars are not equal. Mason jars look similar to the commercial quart and pint-size jars. Genuine Mason jars possess wider rim, which makes them seal better. They come tempered, all owing them to readily resist breaking and cracking under high pressure which is necessary for pressure canning. They have two kinds of mouths; Wide mouth and Regular. Regular-mouth jars come slightly thin, close to the top, enabling them to hold canned foods below liquid level. This type of design is very important for adequate food preservation but not suitable for freezing, on the other hand, wide-mouth jars are suitable for foods that may be hard to scoop in or pour out of regular-mouth jars. Wide- mouth jars are also good for freezing. There are also wide varieties of canning jars, made to preserve all kinds of food.

Wide-Mouth Half-Gall on Jar

These types of jars are used for canning grape juice and apple juice, as recommended by the National Center for Home Food Preservation. Due to their large size, heat penetration is highly negligible. It is, therefore quite impossible to make sure that the food in the center of the jar has been properly heated.

Regular-Mouth Quart Jar
It is conceivably the most effective canning jar. It is suitable for juices, pickles and other chopped fruits and vegetables. It holds the specified amount for use when canning a single recipe, especially if you are pressure canning tomatoes or beans.
Wide-Mouth Quart Jar
This works best for large portions of fruits and vegetables. It is used for freezing as well.
Regular-Mouth Pint Jar
It is one of the widely used canning jars, especially for canning pickles.
12-Ounce Jelly Jar
Though small er than a pint jar (16 oz), it is best for gift giving. You can give
away jellies, or other things, without using much product in one jar.
Half-Pint Jelly Jar
This is also a perfect jar for jellies, and jams preserve, including fruit

butter and very easy to preserve. These varieties may somewhat look confusing because a jar, is a jar but Mason would disagree and so would the USDA. With the recent explosion in interest in home canning, including the present problems of botulism or spoilage, the difference between a fake-Mason jar and a genuine regular-mouth quart jar may perhaps mean the difference between a delicious pickle and a biohazard. Think about it and choose your jars wisely.

Water Bath Canning Tips

Pitfalls to Avoid When Canning
Never use a Pressure Canner when you need to use a boiling water bath.
Remember, acidic foods such as fruit and tomatoes may be preserved safely in a boiling water bath, which does not require any specialized equipment besides a deep, large pot, canning jars, and lids. However, non-acidic foods like meat and poultry must be canned using a pressure canner.
Never Over Fill Your Jars
Always make sure you leave one to ½-inch headspace between the food surface top and the rim of the jar. Do not Fill the jars too high, the lids will not seal if you do. In addition, if anyone remains unsealed, you can keep it in the refrigerator for about one week or eat it immediately. You could also reprocess it, leaving enough headspace and new lids, though much time would be spent. Therefore, it is better to leave the specified free space from the beginning. Always Remember to Adjust the Pressure or Canning time in case of a change in Altitude
Water does not boil at the same time and temperature at sea level as it does at high altitudes. Hence, the need to adjust both the pressure and canning time to ensure adequate food preservation.
Always Use Enough Water in a Boiling Water Bath
When using a boiling water bath/canner, the lids of the jars should be covered by one to two inches of water. This enables food to be heated evenly.
Never Move Jars Before Cooling Down
The moment the jars get out of the water, the cooling process has started, but for it to completely cool down, they must be kept undisturbed to avoid the hot food making contact with the lids'

adhesive seal. That could lead to unsealed jars.

Never Use Cracked or Chipped Jars
Carefully inspect your canning jars. Check for cracks on the jar, as well as small chips around the rim. If not properly checked, it could lead to unsealed jars or jars breaking in the canner.

Never Use Sub-Standard Ingredients
Always use the best ingredients you can get. Tomato sauce taste and smell good as the tomatoes that you began with; a pickle is certainly going to be as crunchy as the type of cucumber that went into it.

Dos and Don'ts
Do invest in a water bath canner.
Don't forget to use new jars without any nicks, chips, or cracks. Do Boil jars and lids before Filling them with food.
Do use the correct jar size for your recipe. If it can't fit in a hot water bath canner, it can't be canned by boiling water.
Do make sure that your jars are completely dry before you Fill them with food.
Do process all foods according to USDA guidelines and always use pressure cookers (if applicable).
Do use canning tongs whenever you are reaching into the hot water bath to remove jars.
Do use the correct procedures, weights, and measurements every time when you are canning your own products at home.
Do use a wide mouth canning funnel or suction canning funnel, to make sure your food is processed in the right amount by avoiding overfilling of jars.
Do write the date on each jar for easier identification if it is contaminated – bacteria can grow if left undated for an extended period of time.
Be sure to consult your canning books and follow the **Directions** in them closely so your batch is successful!
Do check out the USDA guide if you want more information on home- canning, and make sure you read it thoroughly before facing the challenge of home canning on your own.
Don't neglect to sterilize your utensils by boiling them for 10-15 minutes first.
Don't forget to get the right jar lids, and use them only once!
Don't try to Fill hot jars with cold or warm food – they will break when

the contents expand as they are processed in a boiling water bath. Don't process jars that haven't sealed within the specified time according to USDA guidelines.
Don't use old or outdated food recipes. Check out updated canning books and follow their **Directions** carefully.
Never leave food in a hot water bath too long (over an hour). If this occurs, the food will be ruined and smell awful!
Don't Fill a jar more than 1/2 full of food since this can cause spoilage.
Don't forget to add 1/2 cup of lemon juice or vinegar to each quart of jar you Fill. The acidity in this helps to prevent botulism from forming.
Don't Wash inside and outside of hot jars before you put them on the shelf.
Don't use old equipment on new products since they may be contaminated from previous canning adventures.
Don't let jar rims touch the sides of the saucepan since you will have trouble sealing them.
Don't Fill jars with too much food. It's better for small batches instead of large ones since small batches lose fewer nutrients and flavor. Also, a small er amount is easier to process.
Quick tips on Changes and Substitutions in Home Canning
Home Canning and puréeing hot peppers, including jalapeño & cayenne is safe and can be done before Filling jars.
Do use low-sodium canned foods as opposed to making your own since you know how to do it right.
Do warm the jars in hot water bath after sealing and Cooking.
Do process quarts instead of pints since quarts hold more food than pints. It's better to Check food seals in small er jars than it is in larger ones!
Do plan ahead and make sure you have the right equipment lined up before you start with your canning.
Be sure to read the safety section of the USDA's website before you begin.

Canning fruit

Sugar is added to canned fruits help preserve color, help firm texture, and for flavor. Choose a light fruit juice such as white grape juice for canning if you wish to reduce sugar in home canned fruit. Instead of light syrup, use fresh fruit juice to add extra flavor and nutrition.

For whole fruits and berries, Add teaspoon of ascorbic acid per quart jar or two tablespoons lemon juice to prevent darkening.
If you are canning mixed fruit, add 1 teaspoon of citric acid per quart jar or a tablespoon of lemon juice to control darkening.

For jams and jellies, do not add fruit pectin with the fruit to avoid curdling during Cooking. Instead, Add pectin after cooking and before Filling the jars and Cooking.

Be sure that your pectin is low or no-sugar type for safe canning. Most fruits and vegetables freeze well by simple freezing (or pickling) first, then canning as directed in a recipe.

Canning Vegetables

Check out recipes and USDA recommendations for vegetable canning safety. Use only recommended canning methods for your specific food item.

Always pay attention to the recommended canning times specified in home canning books or on the internet.

Use low-sodium vegetable and fruit juice concentrate to replace sugar in canned foods.

Add vinegar to the canning jar(s) as a conditioner and/or preservative. Blanch vegetables first before adding them to the boiling water bath.

Use chipping or chopping methods to freeze vegetables, as opposed to grinding.

Canning Meat

Use a pressure canner for meats and poultry since it is the safest way to can foods.

Be sure to process meats and poultry at least 10 minutes longer than specified in your home canned meat recipe for safety.
All ow more time for cooking meats that are tough since they take longer to soften.

Be sure you cool the meat and poultry thoroughly before you Add m to your jars, especially if using a hot water bath method.
Include only natural spices or seasonings like salt, citric acid, and pickling spices, without added sugar or preservatives, in your home canned foods as well.

Be sure to properly wash and peel all organic foods before you begin.

When canning hot recipes, be sure that the food and jars are all at room temperature before beginning.

Always use a rack in the water bath canner to prevent food pieces from floating to the top of your jar during Cooking.

Canning Salsa

Salsa is a fave among home canning enthusiasts and for good reason! It's easy to can, has a great shelf life, and the recipes are endless! For those interested in learning how to can salsa, there are a few things you should know first. Here are some uncomplicated tips that will help make your salsa extra yummy:
Use fresh ingredients. Purchasing high-quality ingredients is key when it comes to creating a flavorful salsa. You want your salsa to be as natural as possible so stick with fresh ingredients like tomatoes, onions, garlic and spices.

Don't add water. Adding extra water will dilute the flavor of your salsa. If you don't want your salsa to be too watery, Remove water from your tomato before blending it into the salsa.

Add salt. Salt helps bring out the natural flavors in foods like tomatoes, as well as preserve them for longer periods of time. If you taste your salsa and think it is lacking in seasoning, Add little more salt to the mix and tasteagain.

Use a blender or food processor to blend ingredients before canning them. Many recipes call for canned tomatoes but if your tomato still tastes fresh after blending, save those mouth-watering chunks of tomatoes to use later in other dishes and recipes.

Canning Tomatoes

Tomato is one of the staple ingredients in most of the canning recipes out there today. It's affordable, nutritious and delicious. Because tomatoes are a favorite among home canners, here are some tips to help you in your tomato- canning ventures:

Always use fresh, ripe tomatoes. You want your tomatoes to taste good because that's what you're putting into your food!

Use fresh herbs for added flavor. Dried seasonings often do not give your foods the flavor that you're looking for. However, fresh herbs will taste amazing in your canned food.

Blanch tomatoes to prevent them from breaking during the canning process.

If your tomatoes are too juicy after blanching, simply squeeze the juice out of them before adding to the jar.

Homemade Pickles and Relishes

Canned pickles are a favorite among home canners. They have a long shelf life, taste great and are easy to make. When canning your own pickles here are some tips to help you along:

Always use fresh cucumbers. You want the cucumbers to be crisp and flavorful for your canning recipe.

Use at least one clove of garlic per quart of pickles when canning.

Store your pickles in an airtight glass jar in the fridge once they've been cooled down. Canned pickles last up to 2 years if stored properly in a cool, dark place.

Don't add extra ingredients until after the initial Cooking has finished so that you get accurate cooking times and correct level of doneness.

Use the "Boiling Water Bath" Method for canning of pickles. I cannot say this more emphatically. There are many methods to canning pickles, but these are the only ones that truly work.
If your pickles become soft again after being processed (if they look like they have started to melt), simply Place m in a hot oven until the pickles are crisp and crunchy again.
Before using your canned pickle, store it at room temperature for 24 hours so that it is fully absorbing flavors from the jar.
A good rule of thumb when canning is to have one inch of headspace for every one-pint jar that you're canning.

Making Jams and Jellies

Making your very own preserves or sweet spreads can seem like a daunting task to the beginner, especially when you are taking in the different methods and instructions from other recipes. Here are some tips on how to make jams and jellies that won't require you to double-check your calculations for the umpteenth time:

When making jams and jellies, use fresh ingredients. Most people just don't get it, but you really do get what you pay for when it comes to preserving fruits. Fresh ingredients, cooked at the right temperatures, are the only way to ensure that your preserve will have the delicious flavor you're looking for.

Use fresh fruit and vegetables. You don't want to use fruits and vegetables that have been relabeled for preservation or have strange chemicals in them. If you are home canning, then you should use freshly chopped or blended ingredients.

Don't add extra ingredients during Cooking as it can affect the size of your preserves once they are canned.

When making jams and jellies, always follow specific instructions on what temperature to bring your jars up to before Cooking them. Always use a canner, even when making recipes that require no Cooking. Jam or jelly making can be dangerous, so if you feel like your kitchen will be safe and secure, a canner is the way to go.
Don't let your jam boil over as this will cause it to become very runny and cause it to split on top. If you run out of time and need to can something quickly, simply heat the jam up beforehand.

Common Mistakes Made in Canning

After reading all of the canning tips and tricks that I've offered you thus far, it's important to know what the most common problems are when working with home-canned foods. Knowing these common mistakes will help you avoid them altogether and make sure that the food that you put in your pantry lasts for many months to come. While canning isn't exactly rocket science, there are a few things that can go wrong when you can foods at home. Here are some mistakes you should avoid when you're trying to preserve your food:
Not washing your jars and lids with soap and water before use

Leaving foods in the jar after Cooking so that they are not completely processed *Using glass jars that have artificial seams on the rims, because this causes the glass to break more easily during Cooking.

Reusing jars and lids after using for shop-bought products, because this can cause the glass to become too fragile to put in your own canned products and use.

Using metal tools when you are canning as this may scratch your glass jars and cause them to break during Cooking or storage.
Using your canning jars for other purposes such as bath or candle holders. This leads to lighter-colored glass and can cause an uneven seal after Cooking.

Using too high of a water temperature for the cooking time, this can cause the jars to crack during Cooking or when holding in your pantry.

Not adding your jar lids once you've processed them. This also causes jars to crack during Cooking, so be sure that you've sealed them all before storing it in the pantry for a prolonged period of time.

Not Cooking your jars in an actual canner, this can cause jars to break during Cooking or after they've been stored in the pantry.

Using too high of a cooking temperature when you are home canning. This leads to jars breaking and being unsafe to eat after they've been processed.

Not using wooden lids when you are home canning as these do not seal properly as glass lids do.

VEGETARIAN

Chunky Zucchini Pickles

Preparation time: 85 minutes
Cooking time: 35 minutes
Servings: 4 pints

Ingredients:

- 14 cups seeded, unpeeled zucchini (I peeled half of them because this zucchini was huge and the skin was tougher than small er zucchini)
- 6 cups finely chopped onions
- 1/4 cup pickling or canning salt
- 3 cups granulated sugar
- 4 tbsp. Clearjel (I have never seen this in stores but you can purchase it online ~ I used 2 tbsp. of corn starch)
- 1/4 cup dry mustard
- 1 tbsp. ground ginger
- 1 tsp. ground turmeric
- 1/2 cup water
- 2 cups white vinegar
- 1 red bell pepper, seeded and finely chopped

Directions:

In a large glass or stainless steel bowl, combine zucchini and onions. Sprinkle with pickling salt, cover, and let stand at room temperature for 1 hour. Transfer to a colander placed over a sink and drain thoroughly. Note: I also rinsed half the mixture because that is what I've done in the past with pickles...but it says DRAIN not rinse. They still seemed salty.
Prepare for water-bath canning. Sterilize jars in the oven on 250F for 30 minutes.
In a large stainless steel saucepan, combine sugar, Clear jel or corn starch, mustard, ginger, and turmeric. Stir dry ingredients well.

Gradually blend in water. Add vinegar and red pepper.
Boil over medium-high heat, stirring frequently to dissolve sugar and prevent lumps from forming. Reduce heat and boil gently, stirring frequently, until mixture thickens about 5 minutes. Add drained zucchini mixture and return to a boil.
Ladle hot zucchini mixture into hot sterilized jars, leaving ½" headspace. Remove air bubbles and adjust headspace, if necessary, by adding more hot zucchini mixture. Wipe rim with a damp paper towel. Place snaps and rings on each jar, screwing bands down until they are fingertip-tight.
Place jars in canner, ensuring they are completely covered with water. Bring to a full rolling boil and process for 10 minutes. When time is up, Turn off heat, remove canner lid and wait 5 minutes before removing jars to a folded towel on the counter.
Check seals, label, and store. Refrigerate any unsealed jars.

Nutrition: Carbohydrates 154.14g; Fat 3.47g; Protein 11.58g; Sodium 395mg; Cholesterol 0mg Calories 683; Sugars 92.02 g;

Sweet Pickle Sticks

Preparation time: 20 minutes
Cooking time: 20 minutes
Servings: 6 pints

Ingredients:

- 6 pints cucumbers
- Boiling water
- 3-3/4 cups white vinegar
- 4 cups sugar
- 3 tbsps. Salt
- 4 tsps. Celery seed
- 3/4 tsp. mustard seed
- 4 tsps. Turmeric

Directions:

Wash and Cut cucumbers into sticks. Pour boiling water over the sticks and let them stand 12 to 14 hours. Drain cucumbers and pack into sterile jars.
In a large pot, Combine vinegar, sugar, salt, celery seed, mustard seed, and turmeric and bring to a boil. Let the pot boil for 5 minutes. Pour boiling mixture over the cucumbers in the jars, leaving a 1/2 inch headspace. Clean the jar rims and Place lids on. Process the jars for 5 minutes in a boiling water bath.

Nutrition: Cholesterol 0mg Calories 188.5 kcal; Fat: 0.3 g; Carbs: 45.2 g; Protein 0.9 g Sugars 68.3g;

Pickled Beets

Preparation time: 85 minutes
Cooking time: 35 minutes
Servings: 4 pints

Ingredients:

- 3 lbs. fresh, small beets
- 2 sugar cups
- 2 water cups
- 2 cider vinegar cups
- 2 cinnamon sticks
- 1 tsp. whole cloves
- 1 tsp. whole all spice

Directions:

Scrub beets and detruncate tops to 1 inch. Put in a Dutch oven and cover with water. Bring to a boil.
Reduce heat and let simmer, covered, until tender, 25-35 minutes.
Remove from water and let cool. Peel beets and cut into fourths.
Place beets in a Dutch oven with vinegar, sugar, and water.
Wrap cinnamon sticks, cloves, and all spice in a double thickness of cheesecloth. Add to beet mixture.
Boil, then reduce heat and cover. Let simmer 10 minutes. Discard spice bag.
Pack beets into four hot sterilized 1-pint jars to within ½-inch of the top.
Carefully Scoop hot liquid over beets, leaving ¼-inch space of the top. Remove air bubbles and if necessary, adjust headspace by adding hot mixture. Wipe rims carefully. Place tops on jars and screw on bands until fingertip tight.
Place jars into canner with boiling water, ensuring that they are completely covered with water. Let boil for 35 minutes. Remove jars and cool.

Nutrition: Carbohydrates 12 g Fat 0 g Protein 1 g Sodium 44 mg Cholesterol 0mg Calories 53 Sugars 95.68g;

Watermelon Pickles

Preparation time: 20 minutes
Cooking time: 30 minutes
Servings: 4 pints

Ingredients:

- 2 pounds watermelon rind
- 4 cups sugar
- 2 cups white vinegar
- 2 cups water
- 1 lemon, washed and sliced thinly
- 1 cinnamon stick
- 1 tbsp. whole cloves

Directions:

Trim dark green and pink flesh from rind; cut into 1" cubes.
Combine 1/4 pickling salt and 1 quart of water.
Heat and stir until salt are dissolved.
Pour saltwater over rind cubes. Leave overnight.
Drain and rinse cubes.
Place in heavy pot or kettle.
Cover with cold water and cook until tender; drain.
Combine sugar, vinegar, water, lemon slices in a heavy pot.
Place cinnamon and cloves in a cheesecloth bag and put bag in vinegar mixture.
Simmer mixture 10 minutes and remove spice bag.
Add rind cubes to vinegar mixture and continue cooking until cubes are translucent.
Pour into hot, sterile, pint jars, dividing syrup evenly, and leaving 1/2- inch head space.
Process jars in a boiling water bath for fifteen minutes.
Nutrition: Cholesterol 0mg Calories 70 kcal; Fat: 0 g; Carbs: 17 g; Protein 0 g

Tomato Marmalade

Preparation time: 15 minutes
Cooking time: 45 minutes
Servings: 72

Ingredients:

- 5 medium ripe tomatoes, peeled and chopped
- 4 cups tart apples; peeled, cored, and chopped
- 2 medium lemons, seeded and chopped finely
- 8 whole cloves
- 6 cups sugar
- 2¼ teaspoons ground ginger

Directions:

In a colander, Place chopped tomatoes to drain.
In a nonreactive saucepan, add tomatoes, apples, and lemons over medium heat and cook for about 15 minutes, stirring occasionally.
Meanwhile, tie the cloves in a cheesecloth.
In the saucepan, add cloves bag, sugar, and ginger and cook until boiling, stirring occasionally.
Now set heat to low and cook for about 40 minutes, stirring frequently.
Remove saucepan of marmalade from heat and discard the clove bag.
In 9 (½-pint) hot sterilized jars, divide the marmalade,
Slide knife around the insides of each jar to remove air bubbles.
Close each jar with a lid and screw on the ring.
Arrange the jars in a boiling water canner and process for about 10 minutes.
Remove jars from water canner and place on wood surface
Cool then press the top of jar's lid to ensure that the seal is tight.
The canned marmalade can be stored in the pantry for up to 1 year.
Nutrition: Cholesterol 0mg Calories 71 Total Fat 0 g Saturated Fat 0 g Sodium 1 mg Total Carbs 18.8 g Fiber 0.4 g Sugar 18.2 g Protein 0.1 g

Tomato Juice

Preparation time: 15 minutes
Cooking time: 15 minutes
Servings: 20

Ingredients:

- 15 pounds tomatoes, chopped finely
- 1 bell pepper, seeded and chopped finely
- 1 large onion, chopped finely
- 4 tablespoons brown sugar
- 1 tablespoon pickling salt
- 1 tablespoon celery salt
- 1 teaspoon paprika

Directions:

In a stainless-steel saucepan, add chopped tomatoes, bell peppers, and onion and cook until boiling.
Through a food miall, press the mixture.
ReTurn liquid into the same saucepan with the remaining ingredients and again bring to a boil.
Cook for about 5 minutes.
In the bottom of 10 (1-pint) hot sterilized jars, divide the juice,
Slide knife around the insides of each jar to remove air bubbles.
Close each jar with a lid and screw on the ring.
Arrange the jars in a boiling water canner and process for about 10 minutes.
Remove jars from water canner and place on wood surface
Cool then , press the top of jar's lid to ensure that the seal is tight.
This canned tomato juice can be preserved in refrigerator for up 4–6 months.

Nutrition: Cholesterol 0mg Calories 73 Total Fat 0.7 g Saturated Fat 0.1 g Sodium 307 mg Total Carbs 16.2 g Fiber 4.4 g Sugar 11.3 g Protein 3.2 g

Green Tomato Salsa

Preparation time: 15 minutes
Cooking time: 45 minutes
Servings: 64

Ingredients:

- 5 pounds green tomatoes, chopped
- 6 yellow onions, chopped
- 3 jalapeño peppers, chopped
- 4 large bell peppers (red and green), chopped
- 6 garlic cloves, minced
- 1 cup fresh cilantro, chopped
- 1 cup fresh lime juice
- ½ cup white vinegar
- 1 tablespoon salt
- ½ tablespoon cumin
- 1 tablespoon dried oregano leaves
- 2 teaspoons ground black pepper
- ¼ teaspoon ground black pepper
- 1–2 teaspoons sugar

Directions:

In a large nonreactive saucepan, Add all of the ingredients over high heat and Bring mixture to a boil, stirring occasionally.
Now adjust the heat to medium-low and simmer, uncovered for about 30–40 minutes, stirring occasionally.
In 8 (1-pint) hot sterilized jars, divide the salsa, .
Slide knife around the insides of each jar to remove air bubbles.
Close each jar with a lid and screw on the ring.
Arrange the jars in a boiling water canner and process for about 15 minutes.
Remove jars from water canner and place on wood surface
Cool then, press the top jar's lid to ensure that the seal is tight.
The canned salsa can be stored in the refrigerator for up to 1 month.

Nutrition: Cholesterol 0mg Calories 15 Total Fat 0.1 g Saturated Fat 0 g Sodium 128 mg Total Carbs 3.3 g Fiber 0.9 g Sugar 1.8 g Protein 0.6 g

Tomato Chutney

Preparation time: 15 minutes
Cooking time: 2 hour 10 minutes
Servings: 64

Ingredients:

- 2½ cups red wine vinegar
- 3¾ cups apple cider vinegar
- 3¾ cups granulated cane sugar
- 3 tablespoons mustard seeds
- 5 teaspoons sea salt
- 2½ teaspoons ground black pepper
- 2 teaspoons red pepper flakes, crushed
- ½ teaspoon paprika
- 5 pounds tomatoes, chopped
- 5 bell peppers (red), seeded and chopped
- 3¾ cups scall ions, chopped

Directions:

In a nonreactive saucepan, add both kinds of vinegar, cane sugar, mustard seeds, salt, ground black pepper, black pepper, red pepper flakes, and paprika over medium-high heat and cook until boiling. Add in the tomatoes, bell peppers, and scall ions and again, bring to a full rolling boil.
Now set the heat to low and cook for about 2 hours, stirring occasionally.
In 5 (1-pint) hot sterilized jars, divide the chutney, .
Slide knife around the insides of each jar to remove air bubbles.
Close each jar with a lid and screw on the ring.
Arrange the jars in a boiling water canner and process for about 15 minutes.
Remove jars from water canner and place on wood surface
Cool then, press the top jar's lid to ensure that the seal is tight.
The canned chutney can be stored in the refrigerator for up to 1 month.

Nutrition: Cholesterol 0mg Calories 61 Total Fat 0.3 g Saturated Fat 0 g Sodium 152 mg Total Carbs 14.3 g Fiber 0.8 g Sugar 12.9 g Protein 0.7 g

Tomato Ketchup

Preparation time: 15 minutes
Cooking time: 1 hour 5 minutes
Servings: 32

Ingredients:

- 4 pounds tomatoes, seeded and quartered
- 1 sweet red pepper, seeded and quartered
- ½ small onion, cut into chunks
- ½ teaspoon whole all spice berries
- ½ teaspoon whole cloves
- 1 cinnamon stick, broken
- Pinch of red pepper flakes
- 1½ cups cider vinegar
- 1 cup brown sugar
- 2 teaspoons dry mustard
- 2 teaspoons salt

Directions:

Place quartered tomatoes, bell peppers, and onions in a food processor in 2 batches and pulse until very finely chopped.
In a cheesecloth, tie the all spice berries, cloves, cinnamon stick, and red pepper flakes.
In a nonreactive saucepan, add tomato mixture, spice bag, vinegar, sugar, mustard, and salt over medium heat and cook until boiling.
Now set the heat to low and cook, uncovered for about 1 hour, stirring occasionally.
Remove saucepan of ketchup from heat and discard the spice bag.
In 4 (1-pint) hot sterilized jars, divide the ketchup, .
Slide knife around the insides of each jar to remove air bubbles.
Close each jar with a lid and screw on the ring.
Arrange the jars in a boiling water canner and process for about 10 minutes.
Remove jars from water canner and place on wood surface
Cool then, press the top jar's lid to ensure that the seal is tight.

Canned ketchup can be stored in the pantry for up to 1 year.
Nutrition: Cholesterol 0mg Calories 32 Total Fat 0.2 g Saturated Fat 0 g Total Carbs 7.2 g Fiber 0.8 g Sugar 6.2 g Protein 0.6 g

Dialled Green Tomatoes

Preparation time: 20 minutes
Cooking time: 15 minutes
Servings: 4 pints

Ingredients:

- 1 clove garlic
- 1 stalk celery
- 1 hot green pepper
- 1 head of dial
- Salt
- Green tomatoes

Directions:

Pack clean, small , green tomatoes (stems left on) into hot, sterile quart jars.
Place all ingredients to the jars
Combine 2 quarts water, 1-quart apple cider vinegar, and 1 cup pickling (kosher) salt.
Bring to a boil.
Fill jars with liquid, leaving 1" head space.
Process jars in a boiling water bath for fifteen minutes.

Nutrition: Cholesterol 0mg Calories 3.1 kcal; Fat: 0 g; Carbs: 1 g; Protein 0 g Sugars 1.87 g

Pickled Green Beans

Preparation time: 20 minutes
Cooking time: 10 minutes
Servings: 4 pints

Ingredients:

- 1¾ lbs. fresh green beans
- 1 tsp. cayenne pepper
- 4 garlic cloves, peeled
- 4 tsp. dial seed
- 2½ cups water
- 2½ cups white vinegar
- ¼ cup canning salt

Directions:

Pack beans into four hot 1-pint jars to within ½-inch of the top.
Add dial seed, cayenne, and garlic to jars.
In a large saucepan, Bring vinegar, water, and salt to a boil.
Carefully Scoop hot liquid over beans, leaving ¼-inch space of the top. Remove air bubbles and if necessary, adjust headspace by adding hot mixture. Wipe rims carefully. Place tops on jars and screw on bands until fingertip tight.
Place jars into canner with boiling water, ensuring that they are completely covered with water. Let boil for 10 minutes. Remove jars and cool.

Nutrition: Carbohydrates 2g; Fat 0g; Protein 1g; Sodium 83mg; Cholesterol 0mg Calories 9 Sugars, total2.22 g

Peppers & Tomato Salsa

Preparation time: 15 minutes
Cooking time: 15 minutes
Servings: 48

Ingredients:

- 10 cups tomatoes; peeled, cored, and chopped
- 5 cups onions, chopped
- 5 cups green bell peppers, seeded and chopped
- 2½ cups jalapeño peppers, seeded and chopped
- 3 garlic cloves, chopped finely
- 2 tablespoons fresh cilantro, chopped finely
- 1¼ cups cider vinegar
- 1 tablespoon salt

Directions:

In a nonreactive saucepan, Add all ingredients over medium-high heat and cook until boiling, stirring continuously.
Now set the heat to low and cook for about 10 minutes, stirring frequently.
In 6 (1-pint) hot sterilized jars, divide the salsa, .
Slide knife around the insides of each jar to remove air bubbles.
Close each jar with a lid and screw on the ring.
Arrange the jars in a boiling water canner and process for about 15 minutes.
Remove jars from water canner and place on wood surface
Cool then, press the top jar's lid to ensure that the seal is tight.
The canned salsa can be stored in the refrigerator for up to 1 month.

Nutrition: Cholesterol 0mg Calories 19 Total Fat 0.2 g Saturated Fat 0 g Sodium 241 mg Total Carbs 3.9 g Fiber 1 g Sugar 2.3 g Protein 0.7 g

Garlic Diall Pickles

Preparation time: 20 minutes
Cooking time: 15 minutes
Servings: 4 pints

Ingredients:

- 3 pounds Kirby cucumbers
- 1-1/2 c. apple cider vinegar
- 1 tsp. red chili flakes
- 2 tsps. Black peppercorns
- 4 tsps. Dial seed
- 8 peeled garlic cloves
- 2 tbsps. Pickling salt
- 1-1/2 c. water

Directions:

1. Wash and dry cucumbers, cutting them into spears. Remove blossom end of cucumbers. In a saucepan combine vinegar, water and salt to make brine. Boil over medium-high heat. Equall y divide the diall seed, garlic cloves, red chili flakes, and black peppercorns between the jars. Pack cucumbers into the canning jars as tightly as you can without crushing them. Pour brine over the cucumbers, Filling jars to1/4 of an inch from top. Tap jars to help remove air bubbles from jars. Wipe rims of jars and secure the lids in place. Add jars to canning pot and boil for 15 minutes. Remove jars and place on towel on counter to cool at room temperature. Once jars have cooled place in fridge. Let the pickles stay for at least one week before eating.

Nutrition: Cholesterol: 0mg; Calories: 5 kcal; Fat: 0 g; Carbs: 12 g; Protein 0 g Sugars, total10 g

Chipotle BBQ Sauce

Preparation time: 15 minutes
Cooking time: 50 minutes
Servings: 48

Ingredients:

- 1 tablespoon olive oil
- ¼ cup onion, chopped finely
- 2 garlic cloves, minced
- 2 cups tomato sauce
- 1½ (12-ounce) cans tomato paste
- 1¾ ounces canned chipotle peppers in adobo sauce
- 1 cup apple cider vinegar
- ½ cup honey
- ½ cup brown sugar
- 1 teaspoon dry mustard
- ½ teaspoons pickling salt
- ½ teaspoon ground black pepper

Directions:

In a nonreactive saucepan, heat olive oil over medium heat and sauté the onion and garlic for about 2–3 minutes.
Add in the remaining ingredients and cook until boiling.
Now set the heat to low and cook for about 15–20 minutes, stirring occasionally.
Remove saucepan of sauce from heat and with an immersion blender, blend until smooth.
Return pan over low heat and cook for about 20–25 minutes, stirring occasionally.
In 6 (½-pint) hot sterilized jars, divide the sauce, .
Slide knife around the insides of each jar to remove air bubbles.
Close each jar with a lid and screw on the ring.
Arrange the jars in a boiling water canner and process for about 20 minutes.
Remove jars from water canner and place on wood surface

Cool then, press the top jar's lid to ensure that the seal is tight. The canned sauce can be stored in the refrigerator for up to 1 year.

Nutrition: Cholesterol 0mg Calories 32 Total Fat 0.4 g Saturated Fat 0.1 g
Sodium 85 mg Total Carbs 7.2 g Fiber 0.7g Sugar 6.2 g Protein 0.7 g

Zucchini Marmalade

Preparation time: 10 minutes
Cooking time: 15 minutes
Servings: 12

Ingredients:

- 4 cups shredded zucchini
- 4.5 oz. erythritol
- 1 orange, peel, cut into segments and remove seeds

Directions:

Add orange segments and orange peel in the food processor and process until chopped.
Add zucchini, erythritol, and orange in a saucepan and Boil over medium heat for 10-15 minutes or until thickened.
Remove pan from heat and cool completely.
Pour marmalade in a clean jar. Seal jar with lid and store in the refrigerator.

Nutrition: Cholesterol 0mg Calories 326 Fat 0.1 g Carbohydrates 86.4 g Sugar 0 g Protein 0.6 g

Carrot Marmalade

Preparation time: 10 minutes
Cooking time: 40 minutes
Servings: 48

Ingredients:

- 2 cups grated carrots
- 2 ½ cups stevia
- 2 cups water
- 1 orange
- 1 lemon

Directions:

Shred orange and lemon in a large saucepan.
Add remaining ingredients into the saucepan and Boil over medium heat.
Reduce heat to low and simmer for 30 minutes or until thickened.
Once marmalade is thickened then Remove pan from heat.
Ladle marmalade into the clean and hot jars. Leave ½-inch headspace. Remove air bubbles.
Seal jars with lids and process in a boiling water bath for 5 minutes.
Remove jars from the water bath and cool completely.
Check seals of jars. Label and store.

Nutrition: Cholesterol 0mg Calories 43 Fat 0 g Carbohydrates 11.3 g Sugar 0 g Protein 0.1 g

Mustard Pickled Vegetables

Preparation time: 20 minutes
Cooking time: 15 minutes
Servings: 4 pints

Ingredients:

- 1 head cauliflower
- 20 small green tomatoes
- 3 green bell peppers
- 4 cups pickling onions
- 24 2" pickling cucumbers
- 1 cup sugar
- 3/4 cup flour
- 1/2 cup dry mustard
- 1 tbsp. turmeric
- 7 cups apple cider vinegar
- 7 cups water
- 1 cup pickling (kosher) salt

Directions:

Wash cauliflower and break into florets.
Wash tomatoes and quarter.
Wash peppers, cut in quarters, remove stem, seeds, and ribs.
Cut into 1/2-inch strips.
Peel onions.
Wash cucumbers, removing stem and blossom ends.
Toss vegetables in large non-reactive bowl or pot with salt.
Pour a quart of water over all , and let stand overnight.
Drain, cover with boiling water, and let stand ten minutes. Drain.
Combine sugar, flour, spices, vinegar, and 3 cups of water.
Cook until thick.
Add vegetables and continue cooking until vegetables are tender-crisp.
Pack into pint jars, dividing liquid evenly, and leaving 1/2-inch head space.

Wipe rims; screw on lids and rings.
Process jars in a boiling water bath for fifteen minutes.

Nutrition: Cholesterol 0mg Calories 10.1 kcal; Fat: 0 g; Carbs: 2 g; Protein 0 g

Spicy Green Tomato Chutney

Preparation time: 15 minutes
Cooking time: 150 minutes
Servings: 3 pints

Ingredients:

- 2-1/2 cups spiced cider vinegar
- 3 cups shall ots, finely chopped
- 2 quarters small green tomatoes, peeled and thinly sliced
- 1 tsp. celery salt
- 4 cups finely chopped apples
- 2 sweet red or green peppers
- Dry, hot chilies (four to six depending on heat strength)
- 2-1/4 cups brown sugar
- 2 cups ripe tomatoes, peeled and chopped
- Salt

Directions:

Combine 2-1/2 cups of apple cider vinegar, 1 stick of cinnamon, 1 teaspoon of all spice, whole cloves, black peppercorns, and & frac12; teaspoon ground nutmeg in a medium ability boiling pot.
Bring fire on, and nearly get it to the boil.
Remove from the heat immediately and all ow to cool down to room temperature.
Strain before applying to the chutney.
Black tomatoes to be peeled:
Place bowl, pot, or kettle in heat-proof.
Pour over boiling water to cover, letting them rest for three minutes.
Pierce peel with a sharp knife's tip and puall off the skin.
Slice very thinly on those tomatoes.
Pour in a colander over a tub, or green tomato slices with salt in a sink plate.
Let them drain for two hours.
In the meantime:
Peel, Chop apples sweet, core, and finely to make 4 cups.

A place to ready for use in acidulated water.
Clean shallots, then finely Chop m to make 3 cups.
Prepare sweet peppers by washing, seeding, halving, and de rib. Place under broiler or over open flames until the skin is charred and fleece away. Remove peppers; slice them thinly.
Place chilies in a bag with cheesecloth.
Rinse green tomatoes at the end of two hours.
Combine green tomato slices, spiced strained vinegar, shall ots, apples, hot chili bag, brown sugar, and celery salt in a large bowl.
Boil, cook for 15 minutes or until most of the liquid has evaporated.
Remove broiled, ripe tomatoes, and sweet peppers.
Simmer for about an hour, until dark.
Remove bag of chili.
Pour into shot glasses, clean the rims, screw the lids and rings together.
Boiling water bath process: pints and quarts 10 minutes in both.

Nutrition: Cholesterol 0mg Calories 236 18.2; Fat: 0 g; Carbs: 22 g; Protein
g Sugars, total106.14 g

Giardiniera

Preparation time: 10 - 20 minutes
Cooking time: 10 Minutes
Servings: 10

Ingredients:

- 2 chopped cauliflowers
- 4 sliced celery ribs
- 4 sliced carrots
- 1¼ lbs. pearl onions
- 4 sliced serrano peppers
- 4 stripped sweet red peppers
- 6 cups white vinegar
- 3½ cups sugar
- 3 cups water
- 4½ tsps. Canning salt
- 1 tbsp. dried oregano
- 1 tbsp. fennel seed
- 10 bay leaves
- 20 whole peppercorns
- 10 sliced garlic cloves

Directions:

In a stockpot, combine sugar, vinegar, water, oregano, fennel seed, and canning salt. Bring to a boil.
Add carrots, cauliflower, onions, and celery. Return to a boil.
Remove from heat and add peppers.
Carefully scoop hot mixture into hot sterilized 1-pint jars, leaving ½-inch headspace.
Add few slices of garlic, a bay leaf, and 2 peppercorns to each jar. Rinse rims carefully. Place tops on the jars and screw on the bands until fingertip tight.
Place jars into the canner with boiling water, ensuring that they are completely covered with water. Let boil for 10 minutes. Remove jars and cool.

Nutrition: Cholesterol 0mg Calories: 15 Carbs: 3g Fat: 0g Protein: 0g Sugars, total39.35 g

Spicy Carrots

Preparation time: 10 - 20 minutes
Cooking time: 30 Minutes
Servings: 3

Ingredients:

- ¼ tsp. salt
- ¾ tsp. all spice
- ¾ tsp. cloves
- ¼ stick cinnamon
- ¼ piece mace
- ½ tsps. Celery seed
- 2 cups cider vinegar, 5% acidity
- 1-cup sugar
- 2 pints carrots

Directions:

Tie the salt and the spices in thin cloth bag. Boil vinegar, sugar, and spices for 15 minutes. Sterilize a quart jar for about 15 minutes in boiling water.
Remove spice bag. Cook fresh carrots until tender but firm and let cool. Heat the vinegar and add ½ cup of the carrot liquid. Add carrots and simmer for 15 minutes.
Pack into sterile jars, being sure the vinegar covers the carrots. Remove any air bubbles and adjust the lids.
Can for ten minutes in a boiling water bath.

Nutrition: Cholesterol 0mg Calories: 71 Fat: 1g Carbs: 16g Protein 2g Sugars 34.3 g

Cabbage with Beans

Preparation time: 10 - 20 minutes
Cooking time: 30 Minutes
Servings: 6

Ingredients:

- 3 tbsps. Extra-virgin olive oil
- 1 diced onion
- 6 minced garlic cloves
- 1 grated ginger
- 2 tbsps. yellow curry powder
- 2 tsps. Paprika
- 2 tsps. Cayenne pepper
- 1 tsp. salt
- 1 sliced cabbage head
- 3 diced tomatoes
- 1 chopped yellow bell pepper
- 1 chopped red bell pepper
- 1 shredded carrot
- 2 cups chicken or vegetable stock
- 1 can great northern beans

Directions:

In a sizable pot, Combine oil, onion, garlic, ginger, curry powder, paprika, cayenne, and salt.
Cook on medium heat for 8 minutes until the onion softens. Add cabbage and mix well to coat. Cook for an additional 5 minutes to slightly soften the cabbage. Add tomatoes, bell peppers, and carrot. Cook for an additional 10 minutes to blend the flavors, stirring often to distribute the flavors.
Add chicken stock and beans, and mix well. Boil as you stir for 10 minutes.
Arrange the hot jars on a cutting board. Using a funnel, Ladle hot cabbage and beans into the jars leaving a 1-inch headspace. Remove any air bubbles and Additional mixture or cabbage liquid if

necessary to maintain the 1-inch headspace.
Rinse jar rims with a warm towel dipped in distilled white vinegar then Seal lids.
Fill 3 quarts of water and add 2 tablespoons distilled white vinegar to the pressure canner.
Arrange the jars in the pressure canner, lock the pressure canner lid, and Boil over high heat.
Let the canner vent for 10 minutes. Close vent and continue heating to reach 11 PSI (dial gauge) and 10 PSI (weighted gauge).
Can the quarts for 90 minutes and pints for 75 minutes.

Nutrition: Cholesterol 0mg Calories: 300.8 Fat: 5.3g Carbs: 54.8g Protein:
Sugars, total8.74 g

Pressure Canned Potatoes

Preparation time: 10 - 20 minutes
Cooking time: 40 Minutes
Servings: 7

Ingredients:
- 6 lbs. cubed white potatoes
- Canning salt

Directions:

Wash jars thoroughly then Place n in a cold oven. Heat it to 250°F. Boil water in a pot. Also, add 4 inches of water in the pressure canner and place it over medium heat.
Add some salt in each jar, then Fill with potatoes, leaving a 1-inch headspace. Pour boiling water in each jar, then use a canning knife to Remove air bubbles from the jars.
Rinse jar rims and Place lids and rings on the jars.
Arrange the jars in the pressure canner and secure the lid according to the manufacture instructions.
Process the jars at 10 pounds for 40 minutes and 35 minutes for pint jars.
Turn off heat and let the canner depressurize before removing the jars. Place jars on a towel, undisturbed, for 24 hours.
Store in a cool dry place.

Nutrition: Cholesterol 0mg Calories: 108 Fat: 0.4g Carbs: 24.5g Protein: 2.5g Sugars, total 5.95 g

Pressure Canned Carrots

Preparation time: 10 - 20 minutes
Cooking time: 40 Minutes
Servings: 7

Ingredients:
- ½ lbs. carrots
- Salt
- Water

Directions:

Wash carrots and trim them. Peel carrots and Wash m again, if you desire.
Slice the carrots into pieces according to your preferences.
Pack the carrots in the jars leaving a 1-inch headspace. Add ½ tablespoon of salt to each jar, then add boiling water to each jar.
Rinse jar rims with a clean, damp towel, and Place lids on the jars. Arrange the jars in the pressure canner and process them for 25 minutes at 10 pounds of pressure.
Let the canner rest and depressurize before removing the jars.

Nutrition: Cholesterol 0mg Calories: 27 Fat: 0.1g Carbs: 6.4g Protein: 2.5g Sugars, total 5.59 g

Celery Soup

Preparation time: 10 minutes
Time: 30 minutes
Servings: 20

Ingredients:

- 1 lb. celery, diced
- 1 onion, diced
- 4 cups vegetable stock
- 1 medium potato, peeled and diced
- 1 tbsp. olive oil
- 1 garlic clove, minced
- ½ cup dry white wine

Directions:

Heat oil in a large pot over medium heat. Add onion, garlic, and celery and sauté until translucent, about 10 minutes. Add wine and stir well.
Add potato, stock, pepper, and salt, and simmer for 5 minutes.
Remove pot from heat.
Add lids and rings. Place jar into the pressure canner.
Process can soup for 10 minutes at 11 lbs. pressure in a pressure canner.
Once done, cool canner, Remove lid and let jars stand for 10 minutes before removing from canner.
Remove carrots jars from canner and Place m on the counter for 1-2 hours.
Check seals of jars. Label and store.

Nutrition: Cholesterol 0mg Calories 27 Fat 1.2 g Carbohydrates 3.7 g Sugar
g Protein 0.5 g

Carrot Soup

Preparation time: 10 minutes
Cooking time: 1 hour 35 minutes
Servings: 12

Ingredients:

- 4 lbs. carrots, washed, peeled & sliced
- 1 lb. fennel bulb, chopped
- 1 tsp dried thyme
- 2 tsp onion powder
- 12 cups vegetable stock
- 1 tbsp. olive oil
- 1/2 tsp ground cumin
- 1 tsp ground black pepper
- 1 tsp ground coriander
- 1 tsp ground ginger
- 2 tbsp. salt

Directions:

Heat oil in a saucepan over medium heat.
Add fennel and sauté until translucent.
Add carrots and 4 cups of stock and simmer for 30 minutes.
Remove saucepan from heat and using blender puree the carrots until smooth.
Return saucepan on heat.
Add remaining ingredients and stir well and cook on low heat for 20- 30 minutes.
Ladle soup into the clean jars. Leave 1-inch headspace.
Seal jar with lids. Process in a water bath canner for 40 minutes.
Remove jars from the water bath and cool completely.
Check seals of jars. Label and store.

Nutrition: Cholesterol 0mg Calories 86 Fat 1 g Carbohydrates 18 g Sugar 7 g Protein 2 g

FRUITS

Peach Salsa

Preparation time: 15 minutes
Cooking time: 15 minutes
Servings: 32
Ingredients:
- 6 cups peaches; peeled, pitted, and chopped
- ½ cup white vinegar
- 1¼ cups onion, chopped finely
- 7 ounces red bell pepper, seeded and chopped
- ½ cup fresh cilantro, chopped finely
- 4 jalapeño peppers, seeded and chopped
- 1 garlic clove, minced
- 2 tablespoons honey
- 2 tablespoons fresh lime juice
- 1½ teaspoons ground cumin
- ½ teaspoon cayenne pepper

Directions:
Cook peaches, vinegar and remaining ingredients until boiling
Now set the heat to low and cook, uncovered for about 5–10 minutes, stirring frequently.
In 8 (½-pint) hot sterilized jars, divide the salsa, .
Slide knife around the insides of each jar to remove air bubbles.
Close each jar with a lid and screw on the ring.
Arrange the jars in a boiling water canner and process for about 15 minutes.
Remove jars from water canner and place on wood surface
Cool then, press the top jar's lid to ensure that the seal is tight.
The canned salsa can be stored in the refrigerator for up to 1 month.
Nutrition: Cholesterol 0mg Calories 27 Total Fat 0.2 g Saturated Fat 0 g Sodium 47 mg Total Carbs 6.4 g Fiber 1 g Sugar 5.3 g, Protein 0.6 g

Peach Tomato Salsa

Preparation time: 10 minutes
Cooking time: 10 minutes
Servings: 16
Ingredients:
- 2 peaches, peel & chopped
- 1/8 tsp pepper
- 2 tsp brown sugar
- ½ tsp lime juice
- 2 tsp vinegar
- 4 oz. green chilies, chopped
- 1 garlic clove, minced
- ½ tbsp. dried cilantro
- ¼ onion, chopped
- 1 tomato, chopped
- ¼ tsp salt

Directions:
Add all ingredients into the large mixing bowl and mix well.
Ladle salsa in a clean jar. Seal jar with lid and store in the refrigerator.
Nutrition: Cholesterol 0mg Calories 34 Fat 0.5 g Carbohydrates 7.5 g Sugar
g Protein 1 g

Apple & Tomatillo Salsa

Preparation time: 15 minutes
Cooking time: 20 minutes
Servings: 40
Ingredients:
- 4 cups tomatillos, husks removed and chopped roughly
- 2 cups apples, cored and chopped finely
- ½ cup sweet pepper, seeded and chopped
- 1/3 cup jalapeño peppers, chopped
- ½ cup apple cider vinegar
- ¼ cup sugar
- 1 teaspoon salt

Directions:
Cook all ingredients until boiling, stirring continuously.
Set heat to low and cook for about 15 minutes, stirring occasionally.
In 5 (½-pint) hot sterilized jars, divide the salsa, .
Slide knife around the insides of each jar to remove air bubbles.
Close each jar with a lid and screw on the ring.
Arrange the jars in a boiling water canner and process for about 15 minutes.
Remove jars from water canner and place on wood surface
Cool then, press the top jar's lid to ensure that the seal is tight.
The canned salsa can be stored in the refrigerator for up to 1 month.
Nutrition: Cholesterol 0mg Calories 16 Total Fat 0.2 g Saturated Fat 0 g Sodium 73 mg Total Carbs 3.7 g Fiber 0.6 g Sugar 2.5 g Protein 0.2 g

Grape Jelly

Preparation time: 30 Minutes
Cooking time: 30 Minutes
Servings: 32 Servings
Ingredients:
- 3 ½ pounds grapes
- ½ (6 fluid ounce) container liquid pectin
- 7 cups white sugar
- ½ cup water

Directions:
Wash grapes and crush them in a large bowl; transfer to a pan and add in water.
Boil and simmer for about 10 minutes; remove from heat and then extract the juice.
Let juice cool overnight.
Strain juice into a pot and stir in sugar.
Boil and then remove from heat.
Divide among the sterile jars and process for about 5 minutes in a hot water bath.
Nutrition: Calories: 101; Total Fat: 0.1 g; Carbs: 26.2 g; Dietary Fiber: 0.3 g; Sugars: 25.9 g; Protein: 0.2 g; Sodium: 0.7 mg;

Strawberry and Cream Quinoa Porridge

Preparation time: 25 minutes
Dehydrating Time: 8 Hours
Servings: 2 servings
Ingredients:
- 2 c. water
- 1 c. quinoa
- ⅛ tsp. sea salt
- 3 tbsp. cinnamon powder
- 1 tsp. vanilla extract
- ½ lb. strawberries
- ¼ c. coconut milk (powder)
- ¼ c. coconut flakes

Directions:
Wash quinoa with fresh water by rinsing. Take a pot and add that washed quinoa. Now, Add salt to the pot and Wait for boiling of the water.
When it starts boiling, partially Cover pot and keep it on low flame for simmering. Let the pot be like this for half an hour with intermittent stirring. If the water level in the pot drops, you can add more water.
After half an hour, Remove pot from the bear and add cinnamon powder, maple syrup, and vanilla extract. Stir the mixture for a minute to mix all the ingredients.
Now, take washed strawberries and slice them carefully into thin pieces. Put them on the tray in a proper arrangement.
When quinoa is cooked, use a spoon to layer it in the tray. Make sure to line the dehydrator tray with parchment paper.
Set dehydrator at 135 F and let the strawberries and quinoa dry.
Now take an airtight container or bag and put dried ingredients with coconut flakes and coconut milk powder.
Nutrition: Carbohydrates: 99 g; Calories: 630; Fats: 22 g; Protein: 14 g.

Mango Pineapple Salsa

Preparation time: 10 minutes
Cooking time: 30 minutes
Servings: 4
Ingredients:
- 2 mangoes, peeled and chopped
- 2 jalapenos, chopped
- 1 sweet pepper, chopped
- 1 onion, chopped
- 2 garlic cloves, minced
- 1 tsp ginger, grated
- 1/4 cup vinegar
- 1/4 cup lime juice
- 1/3 cup sugar
- 3 cups pineapple, chopped
- 1/2 lbs. tomatoes, cored and chopped
- 1/2 tsp salt

Directions:
Add all ingredients into the large pot and bring to boil.
Reduce heat and simmer for 10 minutes. Stir frequently.
Remove pot from heat. Ladle salsa into the clean jars. Leave 1/2-inch headspace.
Seal jar with lids. Process in a water bath canner for 20 minutes.
Remove jars from the water bath and cool completely.
Check seals of jars. Label and store.
Nutrition: Cholesterol 0mg Calories 280 Fat 1 g Carbohydrates 70 g Sugar 60 g Protein 4 g

Pear Caramel Sauce

Preparation time: 15 minutes
Cooking time: 30 minutes
Servings: 32
Ingredients:
- 2 pounds ripe pears, cored and cut into pieces
- 2 teaspoons vanilla bean paste
- 1 teaspoon sea salt
- 1¾ cups water, divided
- 3 cups granulated sugar

Directions:
Blend chopped pears, vanilla bean paste, salt, and ¼ cup of water until smooth.
Transfer pear puree into a bowl and set aside.
Simmer sugar and remaining water about 15–20 minutes
Remove saucepan of sugar syrup from heat and stir in the pear puree.
Return saucepan over medium-low heat and cook for about 5–10 minutes or until the temperature of caramel sauce reaches between 215°F–225°F, stirring continuously.
In 4 (½-pint) hot sterilized jars, divide the sauce, .
Slide knife around the insides of each jar to remove air bubbles.
Close each jar with a lid and screw on the ring.
Arrange the jars in a boiling water canner and process for about 10 minutes.
Remove jars from water canner and place on wood surface
Cool then, press the top jar's lid to ensure that the seal is tight.
The canned sauce can be stored in the refrigerator for up to 1 year.
Nutrition: Cholesterol 0mg Calories 87 Total Fat 0 g Saturated Fat 0 g Sodium 58 mg Total Carbs 23.1 g Fiber 0.9 g Sugar 21.5 g Protein 0.1 g

Sweet & Spicy Pear Salsa

Preparation time: 10 minutes
Cooking time: 1 hour 20 minutes
Servings: 14
Ingredients:
- 10 tomatoes, chopped
- 1 tsp red pepper flakes
- 1 tsp dry mustard
- 1 tsp oregano
- 2 tsp paprika
- ½ cup vinegar
- ½ cup sugar
- 4 garlic cloves, minced
- 3 red peppers, chopped
- 3 green peppers, chopped
- 2 cups onion, chopped
- 6 cups pear, peeled and chopped
- 1 tbsp. salt

Directions:
Add all ingredients into the large stockpot. Bring to boil, reduce heat to medium-high, and cook for 20 minutes.
Reduce heat to medium-low and simmer for 60 minutes.
Remove pot from heat. Ladle salsa into the clean and hot jars.
Seal jar with lid and store in the refrigerator.
Nutrition: Cholesterol 0mg Calories 104 Fat 0.5 g Carbohydrates 25.4 g Sugar 18.1 g Protein 1.8 g

Chocolate Sauce

Preparation time: 10 minutes
Cooking time: 20 minutes
Servings: 48
Ingredients:
- 3 cups sugar
- 1½ cups water
- 1½ cups Dutch-processed cocoa powder
- 2 tablespoons light corn syrup
- 1 tablespoon vanilla extract
- ¼ teaspoon salt

Directions:
Cook sugar and water until boiling.
Add cocoa powder, corn syrup, vanilla extract, and salt and with a wire whisk, beat until well combined.
Cook for about 14–15 minutes, stirring frequently.
In 3 (1-pint) hot sterilized jars, divide the sauce, .
Slide knife around the insides of each jar to remove air bubbles.
Close each jar with a lid and screw on the ring.
Arrange jars in a boiling water canner and process for about 15 minutes.
Remove jars from water canner and place on wood surface
Cool then, press the top jar's lid to ensure that the seal is tight.
The canned sauce can be stored in the refrigerator for up to 1 month.
Nutrition: Cholesterol 0mg Calories 56 Total Fat 0.4 g Saturated Fat 0.2 g Sodium 13 mg Total Carbs 14.6 g Fiber 0.8 g Sugar 12.8 g Protein 0.5 g

Mango Salsa

Preparation time: 15 minutes
Cooking time: 10 minutes
Servings: 32
Ingredients:

- 6 cups firm mangoes; peeled, pitted, and chopped
- 1½ cups red bell pepper, seeded and chopped
- 1 red onion, chopped finely
- 2 teaspoons fresh cilantro, chopped
- 2 teaspoons fresh ginger, chopped finely
- 2 garlic cloves, minced
- 1¼ cups white vinegar
- ½ cup water
- 1 cup brown sugar
- ½ teaspoon red pepper flakes, crushed

Directions:
Cook all ingredients until boiling
Set heat to low and cook for about 5 minutes.
In 4 (1-pint) hot sterilized jars, divide the salsa, .
Slide knife around the insides of each jar to remove air bubbles.
Close each jar with a lid and screw on the ring.
Arrange jars in a boiling water canner and process for about 15 minutes.
Remove jars from water canner and place on wood surface
Cool then, press the top jar's lid to ensure that the seal is tight. The canned salsa can be stored in the refrigerator for up to 1 month.
Nutrition: Cholesterol 0mg Calories 42 Total Fat 0.2 g Saturated Fat 0 g Sodium 3 mg Total Carbs 10.1 g Fiber 0.7 g Sugar 9.1 g Protein 0.4 g

Cherry BBQ Sauce

Preparation time: 15 minutes
Cooking time: 1 hour
Servings: 40
Ingredients:
- 4 pounds fresh sweet cherries, pitted
- 1 cup onion, chopped
- 3 garlic cloves, minced
- 1 cup apple cider vinegar
- ¾ cup honey
- 3 teaspoons salt
- 2 teaspoons Worcestershire sauce
- 2 teaspoons natural liquid smoke
- 2 teaspoons red chili powder
- 1–2 teaspoons cayenne powder

Directions:
Cook all ingredients cook until boiling, stirring continuously.
Now adjust heat to medium-low and cook, covered for about 15 minutes, stirring occasionally.
Uncover saucepan and cook for about 20–25 minutes, stirring occasionally.
Remove saucepan of sauce from heat and with an immersion blender, blend until smooth.
Return pan over low heat and cook for about 10–15 minutes, stirring occasionally.
In 5 (½-pint) hot sterilized jars, divide the sauce, .
Slide knife around the insides of each jar to remove air bubbles.
Close each jar with a lid and screw on the ring.
Arrange jars in a boiling water canner and process for about 20 minutes.
Remove jars from water canner and place on wood surface
Cool then, press the top jar's lid to ensure that the seal is tight.
The canned sauce can be stored in the refrigerator for up to 1 year.
Nutrition: Cholesterol 0mg Calories 62 Total Fat 0.1 g Saturated Fat 0 g Sodium 168 mg Total Carbs 15.3 g Fiber 0.3 g Sugar 5.4 g Protein 0.2 g

Easy Peach Salsa

Preparation time: 15 minutes
Cooking time: 30 minutes
Serving: 4 c.
Ingredients:
- 3 peaches
- 1 red onion
- 2 jalapenos
- ½ c. cilantro
- 1 tsp. kosher salt
- 2 tbsp. lime juice

Directions:
Prepare all ingredients by cutting and slicing them. Take 3 peaches, Wash thoroughly, Cut m in halves, and pit them. Chop one red onion finely and mince the jalapeno peppers. Get fresh cilantro and mince it roughly.

Set your smoker at 200 F by burning pre-soaked applewood chips. Clean the top of the smoker and keep all the peaches while keeping the skin side downwards. Smoke the peaches for 30 minutes. After the time is up, take out the peaches one by one and Keep m on a rack to cool down. Take a sharp knife and Chop m finely.

Get a normal-sized bowl, add onion, peaches, cilantro, and jalapenos. Stir all the ingredients gently to Combine m after adding salt to taste.

Add 2 tablespoons of lime juice and combine it with other ingredients by stirring. You can add more lime or salt if it is not according to your taste.

Add mixture to a jar using a spoon and refrigerate it. Keep this peach salsa in the fridge for 3 to 4 days for increasing texture and flavor.

Nutrition: Calories: 14; Fats: 0.1 g; Sodium: 1 mg; Carbohydrates: 3.3 g;
Protein: 0.3

Fruit Chutney

Preparation time: 15 minutes
Cooking time: 15 minutes
Servings: 3 pints
Ingredients:
- 1 tbsp. canola oil
- 4 cups onion, chopped
- 1 tbsp. garlic, minced
- 8 cups prepared fresh fruits, peeled including pears, peaches, tomatoes and apples
- 1 cup mixed dried fruits, chopped
- 1 cup granulated sugar
- 1 cup white vinegar
- 1 cup water
- 1 tsp. crushed red pepper
- 1 tsp. salt

Directions:
Heat oil and cook the onion about 6 minutes. Add garlic and stir for 30 seconds. Stir in the fresh fruit, dried fruit, sugar, vinegar, water, red pepper flakes, and salt. Boil, stirring often, then reduce heat and simmer for 30 minutes.
Spoon chutney into sterilized jars to within 1/2 inch of the rim. Wipe rims clean and Place lids on each jar. Process jars in a water bath for 15 minutes.
Nutrition: Cholesterol 0mg Calories 47 kcal; Fat: 0 g; Carbs: 11.1 g; Protein 0 g Sugars, total 172.75 g

Curried Apple Chutney

Preparation time: 15 minutes
Cooking time: 15 minutes
Servings: 10 pints
Ingredients:
- 2 quarts apples, peeled, cored and chopped
- 2 pounds raisins
- 4 cups brown sugar
- 1 cup onion, chopped
- 1 cup sweet pepper, chopped
- 3 tbsps. Mustard seed
- 2 tbsps. Ground ginger
- 2 tsps. All spice
- 2 tsps. Curry powder
- 2 tsps. Salt
- 2 hot red peppers, chopped
- 1 clove garlic, minced
- 4 cups vinegar

Directions:
Boil all ingredients and simmer for 1 hour.
Spoon chutney into sterilized jars, leaving a 1/2 inch headspace. Wipe jars' edge rim clean and Add lid. Process jars in a water bath for 10 minutes.
Nutrition: Cholesterol 0mg Calories 23 kcal; Fat: 0 g; Carbs: 11 g; Protein 0 g Sugars, total144.59 g

Cantaloupe Chutney

Preparation time: 15 minutes
Cooking time: 90 minutes
Servings: 3 pints
Ingredients:

- 3 Medium cantaloupes
- 1 pound of dried apricots
- 1 fresh hot chili
- 2 cups of raisins
- 1 tsp. ground cloves
- 1 tsp. ground nutmeg
- 2 tbsps. Salt
- 2 tbsps. Mustard seed
- 1/4 cup fresh ginger, chopped
- 3 cloves garlic
- 4-1/2 cups apple cider vinegar
- 2-1/4 cups brown sugar
- 4 onions
- 1/2 cup orange juice
- 2 tbsps. Orange zest

Directions:
Thinly slice the apricots and put them into a large bowl.
Chop ginger and garlic thinly, and add to the dish.
Stir in chili, seed, and dice, and add to the pot.
Add raisins, cloves, cinnamon, nutmeg, and mustard seeds.
Mix together and set aside.
Combine vinegar and sugar in a non-reactive pot or kettle; Boil over medium heat.
Add mixture to the pot in a bowl and return to a moderate simmer.
Keep simmer for 45 minutes. Do not deck the pot.
Meanwhile, onions are chopped and placed in a bowl.
Cantaloupes fifth, peel, and seed.
Split the fruit into cubes of 1/2
Add onions.
In cup, add orange juice and zest; mix well.
Once the vinegar mixture has ended 45 minutes of cooking time,
Add cantaloupe mixture to the bowl, bring it back to a cooler, and

start cooking for another 45 minutes or until thickened at the simmer.
Pour into hot glasses, clean the rims, screw the lids and rings together.
Boiling water bath process: pints and quarts 10 minutes in both.
Nutrition: Cholesterol 0mg Calories 54 kcal; Fat: 0 g; Carbs: 14 g; Protein 1 g Sugars, total139.47 g

Orange Marmalade

Preparation time: 10 minutes
Cooking time: 45 minutes
Servings: 6
Ingredients:
- 1 lb. oranges, sliced thinly
- 1 tsp vanilla extract
- 1 cup stevia
- 1 cup water

Directions::
Add oranges and remaining ingredients into the saucepan and heat over medium heat. Boil and simmer for 35-40 minutes.
Remove pan from heat and cool completely.
Pour marmalade in a clean jar. Seal jar with lid and store in the refrigerator.
Nutrition: Cholesterol 0mg Calories 163 Fat 0.1 g Carbohydrates 42.3 g Sugar 0 g Protein 0.7 g

Mango Chutney

Preparation time: 15 minutes
Cooking time: 45 minutes
Servings: 4 pints
Ingredients:
- 6 cups sliced green mangos
- 1/2 pound fresh ginger
- 3-1/2 cups currants
- 8 cups sugar
- 2 cups vinegar
- 3 cups ground cayenne pepper
- 1 cup salt

Directions:
Peel ginger and halve it.
Slice one half of the ginger in thin slices; Chop other half of the ginger roughly.
Grind chopped ginger with half of the currants, using a blender or food processor, until well combined. Placed all in a saucepan, except the mangoes.
Cook, over medium heat, for 15 minutes.
Meanwhile, to make 6 cups, cut, halve, pit, and slice green mangos. After 15 minutes of cooking, Add mangos and simmer for another 30 minutes or until the mangos are tender and the mixture has thickened.
Pour into shot glasses, clean the rims, screw the lids and rings together.
Boiling water bath process: pints and quarts 10 minutes in both. **Nutrition**: Cholesterol 0mg Calories 37 kcal; Fat: 0 g; Carbs: 12 g; Protein 0 g Sugars, total236.2 g

Orange Cranberry Chutney

Preparation time: 15 minutes
Cooking time: 20 minutes
Servings: 3 pints
Ingredients:

- White onion, chopped (2 cups)
- White vinegar, distilled, 5% (2 cups)
- Cinnamon sticks (3 pieces)
- Sugar, white (1-1/2 cups)
- Ginger, fresh, peeled, grated (4 teaspoons)
- Cranberries, fresh, whole (24 ounces)
- Raisins, golden (2 cups)
- Sugar, brown, packed (1-1/2 cups)
- Orange juice, bottled (1 cup)

Directions::
Boil all ingredients, reduce then simmer f0r 15 minutes. frequently stir to avoid scorching.
Once chutney is done, discard the cinnamon sticks. Pour chutney into clean and hot Mason jars (half-pint), making sure to leave half an inch of headspace in each.
Get rid of air bubbles in the jars before fitting their rims with the lids. Place in the pressure canner.
Process for ten minutes.
Nutrition: Cholesterol 0mg Calories 72.4 kcal; Fat: 0.1 g; Sugars: 11.5 g Carbs: 18.2 g; Protein 0.3 g

Cherry Rhubarb Jelly

Preparation time: 10 Minutes
Cooking time: 30 Minutes
Servings: 32 Servings
Ingredients:
- 6 cups diced rhubarb
- 4 cups white sugar
- 6 ounces cherry gelatin
- 21 ounces cherry pie Filling

Directions:
Add rhubarb in a bowl and pour in sugar; stir to coat well and then refrigerate, covered, overnight.
Transfer rhubarb mixture to a pot and cook over medium heat, stirring, for about 30 minutes and then remove from heat. Stir in gelatin and cherry pie Filling. Let cool and then pack on jars. Store in the fridge or freezer.
Nutrition: Cholesterol 0mg Calories: 164; Total Fat: 0 g; Carbs: 42.1 g; Dietary Fiber: 0.6 g; Sugars: 31.5 g; Protein: 0.6 g; Sodium: 17 mg

Jalapeno Blackberry Jelly

Preparation time: 30 Minutes
Cooking time: 10 Minutes
Servings: 72 Servings
Ingredients:

- 1 red jalapeno pepper, minced
- 1 green jalapeno pepper, minced
- 4 cups blackberry juice
- 1 (1.75 ounce) package pectin
- ½ cup white sugar
- 1/2 cups white sugar

Directions:
mix ½ cup of sugar and pectin crystals.
Transfer pectin mixture to a saucepan and stir in blackberry juice, jalapenos and bring to a gentle boil. Stir remaining sugar for about 1 minute or until dissolved. Remove from heat and stir for about 5 minutes to remove bubbles and foam. Divide among sterile jars and seal in boiling water bath. Refrigerate.
Nutrition: Cholesterol 0mg Calories: 43; Total Fat: 0.1 g; Carbs: 11.1 g; Dietary Fiber: 0 g; Sugars: 11.1 g; Protein: 0 g; Sodium: 1 mg;

Lemon & Wine Jelly

Preparation time: 10 Minutes
Cooking time: 30 Minutes
Servings: 40 Servings
Ingredients:
- ½ cup fresh lemon juice
- 3 ½ cups wine
- ½ cups white sugar
- 2 ounces dry pectin

Directions:
Combine lemon juice, wine and pectin and bring to a gentle boil.
Stir in sugar and cook for about 2 minutes.
Skim off the foam and ladle into sterile jars.
Seal and process in hot water bath for about 5 minutes.
Nutrition: Cholesterol 0mg Calories: 106; Total Fat: 0 g; Carbs: 23.4 g; Dietary Fiber: 0 g; Sugars: 22.7g; Protein: 0 g; Sodium: 1 mg

Plum Jelly

Preparation time: 10 minutes
Cooking time: 50 minutes
Servings: 16
Ingredients:

- 5 lbs. ripe plums, slice in half & discard pits
- 6 ½ cups sugar
- 1 tbsp. butter, unsalted
- 1/75 oz. pectin
- 1 ½ cups water

Directions::
Boil plums and water. Cover and simmer over medium heat for 10 minutes.
Strain plum juice by straining through a mesh strainer. All ow to drain for 30 minutes. Discard plums.
You will get 5 ½ cups of plum juice.
Pour juice into the pot. Add pectin and stir well and bring to boil. Add sugar and boil Jelly for 1 minute.
Remove pot from heat.
Ladle Jelly into the clean jars. Leave ½-inch headspace.
Remove air bubbles.
Seal jars with lids and process in a boiling water bath for 10 minutes. Remove jars from the water bath and cool completely. Check seals of jars. Label and store.
Nutrition: Calories 320 Fat 0.8 g Carbohydrates 83.8 g Sugar 83.4 g Protein 0.2 g Cholesterol 2 mg

Preserved Fig

Preparation time: 10 minutes
Cooking time: 45 minutes
Servings: 14
Ingredients:
- 6 cups figs, trimmed & roughly cut
- 1 packet liquid pectin
- 1 tsp butter
- 1 tsp lime zest
- ¼ cup lime juice
- ½ cup water
- 7 cups sugar

Directions::
Add all ingredients except liquid pectin into the large pot and let sit for 30 minutes.
After 30 minutes place a pot on heat and bring to boil. Boil for 10 minutes.
Stir in liquid pectin. Stir constantly for 1 minute.
Remove from heat and cool slightly.
Ladle fig into the clean jars, leave ½-inch headspace. Remove air bubbles.
Seal jars with lids and process in a boiling water bath for 20 minutes. Remove jars from the water bath and cool completely.
Check seals of jars. Label and store.
Nutrition: Cholesterol 0mg Calories 591 Fat 1.1 g Carbohydrates 154.6 g Sugar 140.9 g Protein 2.8 g Cholesterol 1 mg

MEAT

Ground Turkey Taco Salad

Preparation time: 10 – 20 minutes
Cooking time: 0 Minutes
Servings: 6
Ingredients:

- ½ lb. ground turkey
- 1 tbsp. olive oil
- 1 tsp. chili powder
- ½ tsp. cumin
- ¼ tsp. garlic powder
- ¼ tsp. salt
- ½ cup salsa
- 2 tbsps. Mashed avocado
- ½ tsp. lemon juice
- 1 cup halved cherry tomatoes
- 3 cups chopped romaine lettuce
- ½ cup whole grain tortilla chips
- ½ cup shredded cheddar cheese, shredded

Directions::
Heat olive oil in a sizable skillet over medium-high heat. Fry ground turkey together with chili powder, cumin, garlic powder, and salt until it is completely cooked.
Put on a clean bowl and cool completely.
Mix mashed avocado with lemon juice.
Spoon salsa equally into 6 pint-sized canning jars, followed by mashed avocado.
Next, layer jars with cooled turkey, tomatoes, and lettuce, and top it off with the broken tortilla chips and shredded cheese.
Nutrition: Cholesterol 0mg Calories: 278 Fats: 17g Carbs: 11g Protein: 23g Sugars 0g

Pot Roast

Preparation time: 15 minutes
Cooking time: 50 minutes **Servings:** 2 1-L (quart) jars
Ingredients:
- 2 lb stewing beef and cut into chunks
- 1 cup chopped onions
- 2 tsp dried thyme
- 2 garlic cloves minced
- 2 bay leaves
- 1 cup beef broth
- 1 cup dry red wine
- 2 tsp salt
- 1 tsp ground black pepper
- 1 cup chopped carrots
- 1 cup diced potatoes
- ½ cup chopped celery

Directions:
sterilize bottles in a pressure canner. Enable bottles to cool before using.
Combine meat, thyme, onions, bay leaves, garlic, broth, and wine. Black pepper and salt to taste. Turn heat on and Close lid. Boil for 10 minutes, then reduce to low heat for another 10 minutes.
Add veggies and cook for a further 5 minutes. Turn heat off.
Fill sterilized bottles with the mixture.
Pop air bubbles in the lid and seal it.
Fill pressure canner with the jars. Fill pressure canner halfway with water and process for 25 minutes.
Nutrition: Calories: 23 kcal Carbohydrates: 9.3 g Protein: 34.2 g Fat: 6.2 g

Beef Stroganoff

Preparation time: 15 minutes
Cooking time: 50 minutes
Servings: 2 x liter (quart) jars
Ingredients:
- 1 tsp black pepper
- 2 tsp salt
- 2 tsp thyme
- 2 tsp parsley
- 4 tbsp Worcestershire sauce
- 2 garlic cloves minced
- 1 cup mushrooms sliced
- 1 cup onion chopped
- 2 lb stewing beef
- 4 cups beef broth

Directions:
Sterilize bottles in a pressure canner. cool before using.
combine all ingredients and Boil for 5 minutes. Reduce heat to low and continue to cook for another 20 minutes. All ow cooling slightly after turning off the heat.
Fill sterilized bottles with the mixture.
Eliminate air bubbles from the lid and close it.
Fill pressure canner with the jars. Fill pressure canner halfway with water and process for 25 minutes.
Nutrition Calories: 20 kcal Carbohydrates: 5.1 g Protein: 33.5 g Fat: 6.1 g

Canning Beef

Preparation time: 30 minutes
Cooking time: 1 hour 30 minutes
Servings: varies
Ingredients:
- Canning liquid (Tomato juice, Broth or water) enough to cover beef 5 lbs Beef (Ground beef or cubed chunks)

Directions:
Whether this is ground beef, beef cubes, or beef strips, brown them all . With a slotted spoon, Take meat from the pan, squeezing away much as fat as possible.
Bring canning liquid to a boil and keep it warm while the meat is browning. Water, broth, and tomato juice all are viable alternatives.
Brown meat and pack it into pint or quart canning jars, all owing 1-inch headspace.
Fill the jars halfway with boiling canning liquid, leaving 1 inch of headspace.
Wipe rims and finger-tighten using 2-part canning lids.
Fill jars with water and Place m in the preheated pressure canner. Seal top and let the steam escape for 10 minutes.
Add canning weight (for weighted gauge) after the steam has vented for 10 minutes to enable the canner to begin bringing up to pressure.
Process jars for 1hour for pints and 90 minutes for quarts until the canner reaches target pressure (see notes, since target pressure varies depending on elevation).
Turn off heat and let the canner cool fully once the jars have processed. Remove jars and unSeal canner after it has cooled.
Seals should be checked, rings should be removed, and jars should be washed. Refrigerate any jars that haven't been sealed for immediate use. If properly pressure canned, sealed jars should Keep ir quality for 12–18 months on the pantry shelf.
Nutrition Calories: 1 kcal Carbohydrates: 3 g Protein: 0 g Fat: 0 g

Chipotle Beef

Preparation time: 15 minutes
Cooking time: 48 minutes
Servings: 2 x 1-liter (quart) jars
Ingredients:
- 2 lb beef brisket and cut into chunks
- 2 tsp salt
- 8 garlic cloves
- 2 cups onion chopped
- 2 tsp oregano
- ½-cup coriander
- 2 Chipotle chilies
- 4 cups beef broth

Directions:
Sterilize bottles in a pressure canner. All ow all bottles to cool before using.
Season meat with salt and pepper in a saucepan. Turn on heat and sear for 3 minutes on both sides. Combine onion and garlic in a mixing bowl. Cook for a further minute. Combine remaining ingredients in a mixing bowl.
Simmer beef for 20 minutes over medium heat with the lid closed. Remove pan from the heat and set it aside to cool slightly.
Fill the bottles with the mixture.
Pop air bubbles in the lid and seal it.
Fill pressure canner with the jars. Fill pressure canner halfway with water and process for 25 minutes.
Nutrition: Calories: 32 kcal Carbohydrates: 5.4 gProtein: 22.9 g Fat: 22.6 g

Canned Goulash

Preparation time: 15 minutes
Cooking time: 45 minutes
Servings: 2 liters (quart) jars
Ingredients:
- 4 lb stewing beef and cut into chunks
- 20 peppercorns
- 3 bay leaves
- 2 tsp caraway seeds
- ⅓ cup vegetable oil
- 3 onions chopped
- 1 tbsp salt
- 6 celery stalks
- 4 carrots, peeled and chopped
- 2 tsp mustard powder
- ½ cup water
- ⅓ cup vinegar

Directions:
Use pressure canner to Sterilize bottles. All ow bottles to cool before using.
Combine meat, bay leaves, peppercorns, and caraway seeds in a mixing dish. All ow meat to marinate for 1 hour in the refrigerator.
Heat oil . Stir in seasoned meat after 1 minute of sautéing the onions until aromatic. Before adding the remainder of the ingredients, season with salt to taste.
Boil for 5 minutes with the lid closed. Cook for 15 minutes on low heat. All ow cooling slightly after turning off the heat.
Fill bottles with the mixture.
Remove air bubbles from the lid and shut it. Fill the pressure canner with the jars. Fill pressure canner halfway with water and process for 25 minutes.
Nutrition Calories: 69 kcal Carbohydrates: 1 g Protein: 2 g Fat: 1 g

Canned Chicken & Gravy

Preparation time: 15 minutes
Cooking time: 35 minutes
Servings: 2 x 1 L (quarts)
Ingredients:
- 2 tsp salt
- 1 cup chopped celery
- 1 cup chopped onion
- 1 cup diced potatoes
- 2 lb boneless chicken breasts
- 4 tbsp white wine
- 2 tsp poultry seasoning
- Chicken stock to Fill the jars,

Directions:
Wash bottles in a pressure canner.
cool before using.
combine all ingredients and cook for 10 minutes on medium-high heat.
Fill bottles with the chicken and veggies. Pour enough broth to completely Cover chicken. All ow for a 12-inch headspace. Close lid after removing the air bubbles. In the pressure canner, Place jars. Fill pressure canner halfway with water, then process for 30 minutes.
Nutrition Calories: 56 kcal Carbohydrates: 7.1 g Protein: 77.7 g Fat: 22.2 g

Canned Pork

Preparation time: 15 minutes
Cooking time: 40 minutes
Servings: 1 varies
Ingredients:
- 2 lb pork chops
- Water enough to cover pork
- Canning salt to taste

Directions:
Cool bottles before using.
Put pork chops inside a pot of boiling water and cook for 15 minutes. Strain cooked pork, then Fill the sterilized bottles with it. Bring water to a boil in a saucepan and add 12 tsp of canning salt per pint of water. To dissolve the salt, stir it in.
Fill bottle halfway with pickling solution to Cover meat. All ow 1-inch of headroom.
Close lid after removing the air bubbles.
Place jars. Fill pressure canner halfway with water and process for 30 minutes.
Nutrition Calories: 37 kcal Carbohydrates: 0 g Protein: 46.7 g Fat: 20.1 g

Chicken Stock

Preparation time: 1 hour
Cooking time: 25 minutes
Servings: varies
Ingredients:
- Water sough to cover chicken
- 5 lbs Chicken bones

Directions:
Remove all flesh from chicken bones or carcasses (Some people choose to roast the bones for 1 hour or so at this stage to get a darker, richer stock.)
EITHER WAY: Fill saucepan halfway with water and Add bones or carcass. Boil , then reduce to low heat and cook for 45 minutes. OR put everything in the pressure cooker. Add more water to completely submerge the bones. Cook on high pressure for 30 minutes (13–15 pounds for most North Americans). A handful of bay leaves added to any technique is a great idea.
Strain into a big basin or tub; pick up more of the loosened meat with a second hand, add to your bag of frozen beef, and chiall the stock overnight.
Scrape all of the fat off the top in the morning and discard it.
Microwave stock until it boils (or pot.) If you used a microwave, take caution while removing the food to avoid a surge.
Pour into ½-liter or 1-liter jars while still hot.
Leave a headspace of 3 cm (1 inch).
Clean rims.
Put lids on the jars and Place in pressure canner.
Nutrition Calories: 1 kcal Carbohydrates: 0.7 g Protein: 0.7 g Fat: 0.6 g

Chicken Taco Meat for Pressure Canning

Preparation time: 30 minutes
Cooking time: 90 minutes
Servings: 7 quarts
Ingredients:
- 14 lbs chicken
- 1 large onion
- 4 Poblano peppers
- ½ tbsp Kosher salt
- 3 tbsp garlic powder
- 1 tbsp ground cumin
- 2 tbsp onion powder
- 3 tbsp chili powder
- 2 tbsp Mexican oregano
- 1–2 tsp cayenne pepper
- Chicken broth or filtered water

Directions:
Wash jars, lids, and rings. Fill pressure canner with water according to the instructions of your computer.
Combine onions, chicken, peppers, and all of the spices and herbs. Uniformly coating
Remove any air bubbles and leave 1-inch headspace in the jars. If necessary, Add little cold water or cold chicken broth to get a 1-inch headspace. Wipe rims and fingertip-tighten lids and rings. Cold jars should be placed in a cold canner.
Process for 90 minutes for quarts and 75 minutes for pints.
Nutrition Calories: 1 kcal Carbohydrates: 3 g Protein: 9 g Fat: 8 g

Burrito Bowl in a Jar

Preparation time: 5 minutes
Cooking time: 10 minutes
Servings: 1
Ingredients:
- 2 tbsp black beans
- 2 tbsp cilantro
- ½ cup cooked rice
- 1 tbsp plain Greek yogurt
- ½ cup chicken breast
- 1 tbsp salsa
- ½ cup grape tomatoes,
- 1 tbsp shredded Mexican blend cheese
- 1 cup lettuce

Directions:
Place dollop of Greek yogurt in the bottom of a 16-oz canning jar, followed by black beans, cilantro, salsa, and rice.
Combine tomatoes, chicken, and cheese, then top with lettuce.
Nutrition Calories: 45 kcal Carbohydrates: 4 g Protein: 3 g Fat: 1 g

Chopped Beef, Pork, Lamb or Sausage

Preparation time: 10 minutes
Cooking time: 1 hour
Servings: 8–9 pints
Ingredients:
- 10 lbs Preferred fresh, chilled meat, chopped/ground
- Meat broth, boiling/water/ tomato juice enough to cover meat
- 1 tsp salt

Directions:
Prepare cold fresh meat by chopping it into tiny bits. If you're using venison, grind it after adding one cup of high-quality pig fat to every 3– 4 cups of deer. If using fresh sausage, season with cayenne salt and pepper.
Make meatball s or patties out of the mixture. Chop cased sausage into 3–4-inch links if using.
Cook meat until it has become a light brown color. If you're using ground beef, cook it without shaping it.
Fill clean and hot Mason jars with cooked meat. Each one is salty (1 tsp).
Bring beef broth to a boil. Fill jars with tomato juice, beef broth, or water until they are 1 inch from the top.
Remove any air bubbles while fitting the lids, then process for 1 hour and 15 minutes (pints) or 1 hour and 30 minutes (quarts) in a pressure canner (quarts).
Nutrition Calories: 64 kcal Carbohydrates: 1 g Protein: 3 g Fat: 5 g

Canned Chile, Corn & Chicken Chowder

Preparation time: 40 minutes
Cooking time: 30 minutes
Servings: 5 quarts
Ingredients:
- 2 Poblano chile peppers
- 1 ½ cup chopped onions
- 2 tbsp vegetable oil
- 1 cup chopped celery
- 12 cups chicken broth
- 2 tsp mild chili powder
- 4 cups chopped cooked chicken
- 5 cups fresh corn kernels
- Mashed potato flakes
- ½ tsp black pepper
- Cheese slices

Directions:
Heat vegetable oil in a 6–8-quart saucepan over medium-high heat. Cook and stir for 3–4 minutes, or until onions, celery, and chilies are softened. Continue cooking for 1 minute after adding the ancho powder.
Combine broth, corn, chicken, and black pepper in a large mixing bowl. Bring water to a boil.
Fill quart canning jars midway with chicken and veggies in a hot, clean kitchen. Fill pot halfway with broth, leaving a 1-inch headroom. Adjust lids and screw bands after wiping jar rims.
Adjust for altitude and process full jars in a pressure canner for 120 minutes at 10 pounds pressure for only a weighted gauge canner and 11 pounds pressure for a dial-gauge canner. Let pressure naturall y decrease. Remove canner lid with care and cool the jars in the canner for 10 minutes. Remove jars from the canner and Place on wire racks to cool. After 24 hours, Check lids for seal.
Place contents from one jar inside a medium pot to serve. Bring water to a quick boil. Cover and cook for 5 minutes (add 1 additional minute for every 1,000 feet of elevation). Remove pan from the heat. Stir in ½ cup quick mashed potato flakes plus two 3/4-ounce broken pieces of American cheese until the cheese melts.
Nutrition Calories: 23 kcal Carbohydrates: 2 g Protein: 1 g Fat: 1 g

Pozole Verde

Preparation time: 1 hour 30 minutes
Cooking time: 30 minutes
Servings: 6-quart jars
Ingredients:
- 12 cups chicken broth
- 2 lb chicken thighs
- 3 15-oz cans golden hominy
- 15 tomatillos
- 1 bunch cilantro
- 2 Poblano chile peppers
- 3 medium onions
- 4 Jalapeño chili peppers
- 3 tbsp honey
- ½ cup orange juice
- 1 tbsp ground cumin
- 1 tbsp Mexican oregano

Directions:
Combine chicken thighs and stock in a 6–8-quart Dutch oven or heavy pot. Boil, then Turn off heat. Cook for 30 minutes, covered. Remove thighs from the soup and shred the meat. Return chicken to the pot and discard the bones.
To the chicken mixture in the pot, add honey, hominy, jalapenos, onions, cilantro, oregano, poblano, orange juice, tomatillos, and cumin. Boil, then reduce to low heat and cook for 5 minutes.
Fill each heated quart canning jar halfway with chicken and veggies. Fill pot halfway with boiling broth, all owing a 1-inch headroom. Set lids and screw bands after wiping jar rims.
Adjust for altitude and process full jars in a pressure canner for 75 minutes at 10 pounds pressure for a weighted gauge canner or 11 pounds pressure for a dial-gauge canner. Let pressure naturall y decrease. Remove canner lid with care and cool the jars in the canner for 10 minutes. Remove jars from the canner and Place m on a wire rack to cool. After 24 hours, Check lids for seal.
Place contents of the jar inside a medium pot to serve. Bring water to a quick boil. Cover and cook for 10 minutes.
Nutrition Calories: 12 kcal Carbohydrates: 1 g Protein: 9 g Fat: 3 g

Chicken Pressure Canner

Preparation time: 20 minutes
Cooking time: 12 hours and 20 minutes
Servings: 1 gall on
Ingredients:
- 1 medium yellow onion
- 2 celerieS ribs
- 5 lb chicken bones
- 2 carrots
- 1 small bay leaf
- 10 peppercorns
- 2 tsp canning salt
- 1 garlic clove
- 1-gall on water
- 1 tsp saffron thread

Directions:
Place all of this in your crockpot on low flame for 12 hours or overnight. If you wish, you can wait a little longer.
Strain everything with a sieve when you're ready to pressure can. Once or twice, strain the stock through many layers of moist paper towels. This will result in a very clear stock that can be de-fatted without having to refrigerate it.
Use in your favorite dish or in the following ways:
Pour into sterilized jars, adjust tops, and process in a pressure canner for 15 minutes for pints and 25 minutes for quarts at 10–11 pounds of pressure.
All ow jars to cool on their own in a draft-free area. Clean the jars, label them, and enjoy.
Nutrition Calories: 37 kcal Carbohydrates: 0 g Protein: 46.7 g Fat: 20.1 g

Canned Chicken and Gravy

Preparation time: 10 Minutes
Cooking time: 35 Minutes
Servings: 5
Ingredients:
- 1 Cup chopped onion
- 1 Cup chopped celery
- 1 Cup diced potatoes
- 2 Pounds boneless chicken breasts
- 2 Teaspoons salt
- 2 Teaspoons poultry seasoning
- 4 Tablespoons white wine
- Enough chicken stock to Fill the jars

Directions::
Sterilize jars in a pressure canner as indicated in the general guidelines of this book. All ow jars to cool.
Place all ingredients in a saucepan and all ow to simmer for 10 minutes over medium high heat.
Put chicken and vegetables into the jars. Pour over enough broth to Cover chicken. Leave a ½ inch headspace.
Remove air bubbles and Close lid.
Place jars in pressure canner. Place in a pressure canner and process for 25 minutes.
Nutrition: Cholesterol 0mg Calories: 562 Cal; Protein: 77.7 g; Sugar: 0 g; Fat: 22.2 g; Carbs: 7.1 g

Chicken and Mushroom Cacciatore

Preparation time: 10 – 20 minutes
Cooking time: 0 Minutes
Servings: 4
Ingredients:
- 4 lbs. chopped chicken breasts and thighs
- 2 cups chopped mixed bell peppers
- 3 quartered onions
- 2 cups sliced mushrooms
- ¼ tsp. salt
- 8 smashed garlic cloves
- 1 bottle red wine
- 4 cups diced tomatoes with juice
- 2 tbsps. Dried oregano
- 2 tbsps. Dried basil
- 2 tbsps. Dried thyme
- ¼ tsp. black pepper

Directions::
Layer chicken, peppers, onions, mushrooms, and garlic in quart jars. Season with salt and pepper.
Boil wine, tomatoes, and herbs in a stock pot. Season with salt and pepper.
Put the hot liquid over the layered ingredients in your jars.
Lid the jars and process them in your pressure canner for 90 minutes at 11 PSI, adjusting for altitude.
Nutrition: Cholesterol 0mg Calories: 223.6 Fat: 15.6g Carbs: 13.1g Protein: 9.0g Sugars 0g

Turkey and Green Beans

Preparation time: 10 – 20 minutes
Cooking time: 0 Minutes
Servings: 4
Ingredients:
- 4 cups shredded cooked turkey
- 2 cups cut green beans
- 1½ cups chopped carrots
- 1 cup sliced onion
- 2 cups chicken or turkey broth

Directions::
Combine turkey, green beans, carrots, onion, and broth. Boil over medium-high heat.
Leave to cook for 5 minutes, then remove from the fire.
Arrange hot jars on a cutting board.
Ladle hot mixture using a funnel into the jars leaving some headspace. Remove any air bubbles and add additional mixture if necessary.
Rinse rim of each jar with a warm cloth dipped in white vinegar.
Add 3 quarts of water and add 2 tbsps. Distilled white vinegar to the pressure canner.
Put jars in the pressure canner, lock the pressure canner lid, and Boil over high heat for 10 minutes.
Process for 90 minutes (quarts) and for 75 minutes (pints).
Let pressure in the canner reach zero then Remove jars after 10 minutes.
Nutrition: Cholesterol 0mg Calories: 202.2 Carbs: 9.6g Fat: 8.6g Protein: 20.3g Sugars 0g

Canned Turkey

Preparation time: 10 Minutes
Cooking time: 35 Minutes
Servings: 5
Ingredients:
- 2 Pounds turkey breasts, sliced into bite-sized pieces
Canning salt
- Water

Directions::
Sterilize jars in a pressure canner as indicated in the general guidelines of this book. All ow jars to cool.
Place turkey breasts in boiling water and all ow to simmer for 10 minutes. Strain cooked turkey and pack them in the sterilized jars. bring water to a boil and add ½ teaspoon canning salt per pint of water. Stir to dissolve salt.
Pour pickling solution into the jar to Cover turkey. Leave an inch of headspace.
Remove air bubbles and Close lid.
Place jars in pressure canner. Place in a pressure canner and process for 25 minutes.
Nutrition: Cholesterol 0mg Calories: 285 Cal; Protein: 39.7 g; Sugar: 0 g; Fat: 12.7 g; Carbs: 0 g

Pressure Canned Rosemary Chicken

Preparation time: 10 – 20 minutes
Cooking time: 0 Minutes
Servings: 10
Ingredients:
- 20 sprigs of rosemary
- 10 lbs. boneless chicken breast
- ¼ cup salt

Directions::
Add sprig of rosemary to each sterilized jar.
Slice chicken breasts into large chunks and pack in the jars leaving a 1.5-inch headspace.
Add sprig of rosemary at the top then Add tbsp. of salt in each jar.
Rinse rims of jar with a clean damp towel, and then Place lids and the rings. Transfer jars to the pressure canner and process them at 10 pounds pressure for 75 minutes.
Wait for pressure canner to depressurize to zero before removing the jars using cooking tongs.
Transfer jars on a cooling rack for 24 hours to Seal n store in a cool dry place.
Nutrition: Cholesterol 0mg Calories: 182.6 Fat: 7.8g Carbs: 1.0g Protein: 18.8g Sugars 0g

Beef Bell Pepper Soup

Preparation time: 15 minutes
Cooking time: 30 minutes
Servings: 6
Ingredients:
- ½ cup freeze-dried ground beef
- ¾ cup instant brown rice
- ¼ cup dried celery
- 1/3 cup dehydrated sliced onion
- 1 cup dehydrated bell peppers
- 1 tbsp. beef bouillon
- 1 tsp. garlic powder
- ¾ cup tomato powder
- ¼ cup freeze dried sausage crumbled
- 9 cups water

Directions::
Add all ingredients except water into the glass jar. Seal jar tightly with lid.
To cook: Add water and jar content to the saucepan and bring to boil.
Reduce heat and simmer for 15-20 minutes.
Serve and enjoy.
Nutrition: Cholesterol 0mg Calories: 171 Fat: 2.3g Protein: 6.9g Carbs: 32.3g Sugar 0 g

Canned Chili Con Carne

Preparation time: 20 Minutes
Cooking time: 1 Hour
Servings: 9
Ingredients:
- 3 Cups pinto bean or red kidney beans, dried and washed
- 5 1/2 Cups water
- 5 Tbsp. Salt, divided
- 3 lbs. Ground beef
- 1 1/2 cups onion, chopped
- 1 Cup pepper, chopped
- 1 Tbsp. Black pepper
- 3-6 Tbsp. Chili powder
- 8 Cups tomatoes, crushed or whole

Directions::
Place beans in a saucepan, 2-quart, then add cold water to 2-3 inches above beans. Cover and refrigerate for about 12-18 hours to soak. Now Drain beans and discard the water.
Place beans in a saucepot with 5 1/2 cups water. Season with 2 tbsp. salt and Boil for about 25 minutes.
Reduce heat to low and simmer for about 30 minutes. Meanwhile, brown the beef with onions and pepper (optional) in a skillet, then Drain fat off.
Add 3 tbsp. salt, and the remaining ingredients together with cooked beans and simmer for about 5 minutes. Make sure not to thicken. Scoop hot chili stew into hot pint jars. Leave a 1 inch headspace. Do not use quart jars.
If needed, Remove air bubbles, adjusting the headspace. Wipe rims of the jars using a clean damp paper towel
Now apply the 2-piece metal caps.
Process pint jars in a pressure canner for about 75 minutes at 11 pounds pressure if using a dial-gauge canner, or a 10 pounds pressure if using a weighted-gauge canner.
Nutrition: Cholesterol 0mg Calories: 556 Cal; Fat: 11.4g; Carbs 51g; Protein: 61.9g; Sugar: 6.7g

Canned Beef Broth

Preparation time: 15 Minutes
Cooking time: 3-4 Hours
Servings: 4
Ingredients:
- Beef bones, trimmed and meat removed
- Optional: 2 quartered onions
- Optional: 2 sliced carrots
- Optional: 2 sliced celery stalks
- Optional: 2 bay leaves
- Salt to taste Water to cover

Directions::
Prepare bones by cracking them to enhance flavor extraction. Now Rinse m.
Now Place bones and optional ingredients, if using in a large stockpot.
Add water to cover everything then Cover pot. Simmer for about 3-4 hours.
Remove and discard bones, vegetables, and bay leaves. Now cool the broth, skim off the fat and discard it.
If desired, season with salt.
Reheat your broth to boiling.
Scoop hot broth into hot quart jars leaving a 1 inch headspace.
Wipe jar rims using a clean and damp paper towel, and then apply the 2- piece metal caps.
Process quart jars in a pressure canner for 25 minutes at 11 pounds pressure if using a dial-gauge canner, or a 10 pounds pressure if using a weighted-gauge canner.
Nutrition: Cholesterol 0mg Calories: 207 Cal; Fat: 7.8g; Fat: 2.9g; Carbs: 9.1g; Protein: 24.3g; Sugar: 3.9g

Pressure Canned Chicken Broth

Preparation time: 10 Minutes
Cooking time: 30-45 Minutes
Servings: 2
Ingredients:
- Chicken carcass bones, meat removed
- Optional: 2 quartered onions
- Optional: 2 sliced celery stalks
- Optional: 2 bay leaves
- Optional: Salt to taste
- Water to cover

Directions::
Place chicken bones and all optional ingredients in a stockpot, large, then add water to cover everything.
Cover pot and simmer for about 30-45 minutes until the remaining meat tidbits fall off easily.
Remove and discard the bones, then strain the broth and discard bay leaves and vegetables.
Cool broth, then skim off the fat and discard it. Season with salt if desired.
Reheat your broth to boiling.
Scoop broth into quart jars. Leave a 1 inch headspace.
Wipe jar rims using a clean damp paper towel, then apply the 2-piece metal caps.
Process quart jars in a pressure canner for 25 minutes at 11 pounds pressure if using a dial-gauge canner, or a 10 pounds pressure if using a weighted-gauge canner.
Nutrition: Cholesterol 0mg Calories: 233 Cal; Fat: 13.1g; Carbs: 12.1g; Protein: 16.5g; Sugars 4.9g

Chicken Tortilla Soup

Preparation time: 10 minutes
Cooking time: 30 minutes
Servings: 6
Ingredients:
- 1 cup dehydrated chicken
- ¼ tsp. ground chipotle pepper
- 1 cup dried corn
- 2/3 cup dried green chilies
- ½ cup dehydrated sliced onion
- 1 tsp. garlic powder
- 2 tsp. chicken bouillon
- 1 ½ tbsp. chili powder
- ½ cup tomato powder
- 8 cups water

Directions::
Add all ingredients into the glass jar. Seal jar tightly with lid and shake well.
To cook: Add water and jar content to the saucepan and bring to boil.
Reduce heat and simmer for 15-20 minutes.
Serve with tortialla chips.
Nutrition: Cholesterol 0mg Calories: 120 Fat: 1.6g Protein: 9.8g Carbs: 19.2g Sugar 0 g

FISH AND SEAFOOD

Pressure Canned Shrimp

Preparation time: 10 – 20 minutes
Cooking time: 0 Minutes
Servings: 10
Ingredients:
- 10 lbs. shrimp
- ¼ cup salt
- 1 cup vinegar

Directions::
Remove heads immediately, then chill until ready to preserve them. Wash shrimp and Drain m well.
Add gall on of water in a pot then add salt and vinegar. Bring to boil, then cook shrimp for 10 minutes.
Remove shrimp from the cooking liquid with a slotted spoon, then rinse in cold water and drain. Peel shrimp while packing them in the sterilized jars.
Add gall on of water with 3 tbsp. salt and bring it to a boil. Add brine to the jars and Remove air bubbles. Add more brine if necessary.
Wipe jar rims with a cloth damped in vinegar. Place lids and the rings.
Process at 10 pounds pressure for 45 minutes.
Wait for pressure canner to depressurize to zero before removing the jars.
Place jars on a cooling rack undisturbed then store in a cool dry place.
Nutrition: Cholesterol 0mg Calories: 100 Fat: 2g Carbs: 1g Protein: 15g Sugar 0 g

Smoked Salmon
Preparation time: 15 minutes
Cooking time: 4 Hours
Servings: 5 lb.
Ingredients:

- 5 lb. salmon (Cher or trout)
- Maple syrup or birch for basting
- 1 qt. of cold water
- ⅓ c. kosher salt
- 1 c. brown sugar

Directions::
Make brine by mixing the ingredients. Take a container made of non- reactive material, Place salmon in it and cover.
Cure the salmon for 4 hours to properly eliminate the moisture and let the salt penetrate it. This step will ensure the long preservation of the salmon.
If you use Fillets or pink salmon, keep it in the brine for 4 hours. But for a whole and large salmon or trout, cure it for 6 to 8 hours. But the maximum time for curing should never exceed 48 hours. After the curing time, take out the salmon and wash it underwater. The water should be cold and running. Rinse it thoroughly and let it dry.
Take a cooling rack and set the salmon Fillets on the rack. Keep fish skin-side towards down in a cold and breezy place with a temperature around 60 F. Keep it in the same place for 2 to 4 hours unless it dries fully. You can refrigerate it for the whole night too.
The fish will develop a pellicle that is the fish's shiny surface. This shiny skin adheres to the smoke because of the stickiness it offers. You can keep this fish in the fridge again before smoking for a better taste.
Take some oil and slick the skin of the salmon. It prevents the Fillets from sticking to the rack. Now set the temperature of the smoker around 120 F. But build a small fire and gradually let the temperature rise to the required level. Let the smoker temperature go 150 F in an hour. And for the last hours, it should be at 175 F. Open the smoker after 1 hour, and baste the salmon with maple syrup, birch, or honey. Repeat this basting step every hour. You will prevent the albumin from building up. The internal temperature of the salmon should be around 140 F. Do not let the temperature go higher than this. Otherwise, salmon will bleed a lot of albumins.

Check salmon if it is smoked fully. Take it out and keep it on a cooling rack. Wait for an hour for the salmon to cool down completely. Now, wrap it in a plastic sheet and keep it in the fridge. This smoked salmon is good to go for 10 hours. It can stay preserved for 3 weeks if you store it by vacuum sealing.
Nutrition: Calories: 132; Protein: 21.3 g; Cholesterol: 26.6 mg; Fats: 4.9 g;
Calcium 10 mg.

Pressure Canned Salmon

Preparation time: 10 – 20 minutes
Cooking time: 0 Minutes
Servings: 6
Ingredients:
- 5 lbs. salmon Salt

Directions::
Eviscerate salmon immediately after catching it then clean it thoroughly with clean water.
Chill it until you are ready to pressure can it. Remove tail, the head, and the fins. Split the fish lengthwise then cut into small pieces that perfectly fit into your jars.
Pack fish in sterilized jars leaving a 1-inch headspace. Add tbsp. of salt in each jar if you desire.
Rinse jar rims with a damp paper towel then Place lids and the rings on the jar.
Pressure-can the jars in the pressure canner at 11 pounds pressure for 100 minutes.
Wait for pressure canner to depressurize to zero before removing the jars.
Transfer jars on a cooling rack for 24 hours then store in a cool dry place.
Nutrition: Cholesterol 0mg Calories: 121 Fat: 5.4g Carbs: 0g Protein: 17g Sugar 0 g

Soy Marinated Salmon Jerky

Preparation time: 10 – 20 minutes
Cooking time: 4 Hours (Dehydration)
Servings: 2
Ingredients:
- 1 lbs. boneless salmon Fillet
- ¼ tsp. salt
- ½ cup apple cider vinegar
- 2 tbsps. Low-sodium soy sauce
- ¼ tsp. black pepper
- 1 tbsp. fresh lemon juice
- 2 tsps. Paprika
- ½ tsp. garlic powder

Directions::
Freeze salmon for about 30 minutes until it is firm.
Meanwhile, whisk apple cider vinegar, soy sauce, and lemon juice in a mixing bowl.
Add paprika and garlic powder, then stir well.
Season salmon with salt and pepper to taste, then Remove skin.
Slice salmon into ¼-inch thick strips, then Place m in a bowl or glass dish.
Pour in marinade, turning to coat, and then cover with plastic and chill for 12 hours.
Drain salmon slices and Place m on paper towels to soak up the extra liquid.
Spread salmon slices on your dehydrator trays in a single layer.
Dry for 3 to 4 hours at 145°F (63°C) until dried, but still tender and chewy.
Cool salmon jerky completely, then store in airtight containers in a cool, dark location.
Nutrition: Cholesterol 0mg Calories: 203 Protein: 20g Fat: 5g Carbs: 27g Sugar 0 g

Ginger Miso Salmon Salad

Preparation time: 10 – 20 minutes
Cooking time: 10 Minutes
Servings: 2
Ingredients:
- 2 tbsps. White miso paste
- 1 tbsp. brown sugar
- 1 tsp. grated ginger
- 1 tbsp. low sodium soy sauce
- 4 oz. salmon Fillet
- 2 shredded carrots
- ½ cup edamame
- ½ diced cucumber
- 8 cups chopped romaine
- ¼ cup roasted peanuts
- Dressing
- 2 tbsps. Rice wine vinegar
- 1 tbsp. sesame oil

Directions::
Preheat oven to 350°F.
Mix miso paste, sugar, ginger, and soy sauce in a small bowl until well combined.
Put salmon Fillet on a baking sheet and drizzle half the miso mixture over the fish.
Transfer salmon in the oven for 8-10 minutes, or until cooked. Remove from oven for cooling.
Break the salmon into large flakes using a fork once cooled.
To make dressing: Incorporate rice wine vinegar and sesame oil into the remaining miso mixture. Spoon equal amounts of the dressing into 2 quart-sized canning jars.
Pile on rest of the ingredients in the following order: carrots, edamame, cucumber, salmon, romaine lettuce, and peanuts.
Cover with lids and you are ready to go.
Nutrition: Cholesterol 0mg Calories: 424 Fats: 25g Carbs: 30g Protein: 37g Sugar 7.08 g

Pressure Canned Tuna

Preparation time: 10 – 20 minutes
Cooking time: 0 Minutes
Servings: 6
Ingredients :
- 5 lbs. tuna Salt

Directions::
Use a sharp kitchen knife to peel off the skin, then scrape the surface to Remove blood vessels.
Cut fish lengthwise, then into pieces that fit into a pint jar.
Add salt in each jar.
If you have precooked the tuna, Add fish, some vegetable oil, and a tbsp. of salt per pint jar.
Clean rims and Place lids and the rings on the jars.
Process at 10 pounds pressure for 100 minutes.
Wait for pressure canner to depressurize to zero before removing the jars.
Transfer jars on a cooling rack for 24 hours, then store in a cool dry place.
Nutrition: Cholesterol 0mg Calories: 191 Fat: 1.4g Carbs: 0g Protein: 42g Sugar 0 g

Canned Tuna

Preparation time: 10 – 20 minutes
Cooking time: 20 Minutes
Servings: 3
Ingredients:
- 3 lbs. tuna
- 2 cups water
- ¼ tsp. salt

Directions::
After removing the viscera, Wash fish thoroughly and drain out all blood.
Slice tuna in crosswise halves. Bake at 250°F for 4 hours, and then put in the refrigerator to all ow the meat to firm up.
Remove skin, blood vessels, discolored/dark flesh, fin bases, and bones. Slice into quarters and add to clean and hot Mason jars, packing firmly in oil or water. Make sure an inch of headspace remains and that all air bubbles are removed from the jars.
Adjust lids and Place m in the pressure canner. Process for one hour and twenty minutes.
Nutrition: Cholesterol 0mg Calories: 104 Sodium: 33 mg Dietary Fiber: 1.4g Total Fat: 4.1g Total Carbs: 16.3g Protein: 1.3g Sugar 0 g

Fish Chowder

Preparation time: 10 – 20 minutes
Cooking time: 30 Minutes
Servings: 8
Ingredients:
- ¾ cup chopped onion
- 3 tbsps. Butter
- ½ cup chopped celery
- 2 cups diced potatoes
- 1 tsp. garlic powder
- 2 cups chicken broth
- 2 diced carrots
- 1 tsp black pepper
- 1 tsp salt
- 32 oz. canned fish
- 1 tsp. dried dial weed
- 15 oz. canned creamed corn
- 12 oz. canned evaporated milk
- ½ lb. shredded cheddar cheese

Directions::
Melt butter.
Cook celery, onion, and garlic powder for 5 minutes in the melted butter.
Stir in carrots, potatoes, salt, broth, pepper, and dial.
Boil, then Reduce heat to low.
Cover and simmer for 20 minutes.
Stir in milk, cheese, corn, and fish.
Cook until cheese melts.
Fill jars with fish chowder to 1/2 inch from the top.
Put jars in the canner and Fill with water up to the jar rings. Close and lock pressure canner and Boil over high heat, then add cooking weight to the top.
After 20 minutes, Turn heat to medium and cook for 75 minutes.
Turn off heat and leave the canner alone until it has cooled completely to room temperature.
After canner has cooled, Remove jars from the canner and check for
sealing.
If the jars have sealed, store for up to 2 years; if not, use the meat right away.
Nutrition: Cholesterol 0mg Calories: 249.0 Fat: 8.1g Carbs: 14.5g Protein: 26.5g Sugar 0 g

Strong Fish Stock

Preparation time: 15 minutes
Cooking time: 45 minutes
Servings: 4 quarts
Ingredients:
- 8 mediums carrots
- 4 mediums onions
- 4 tbsp unsalted butter
- 8 stalks celery
- 2 tbsp black peppercorns
- ½ cup dry white wine
- 4 bay leaves
- 12–16 sprigs fresh thyme
- 8 lb fish bones
- 4 quarts hot water Kosher salt
- A pich of parsley

Directions:
Prepare veggies by slicing the onions crosswise into thin slices. Carrots should be peeled and celery should be sliced.
In a large 12–16-quart stockpot, melt the butter. Cook, stirring periodically, until the veggies soften without browning, Add onions, carrots, celery, bay leaves, parsley, thyme, and peppercorns. This might take anything from 10 minutes.
Place fish frames on top of the vegetables in an even layer. Pour wine, cover, and let sit for 15 to 20 minutes, or until the bones have turned completely white.
Stir in heated water and bring to a gentle simmer over high heat. Reduce heat to low and cook for 10 minutes, stirring occasionally. Remove from the fire, give it a quick stir, and set aside for 15 minutes.
Using a fine strainer, strain the stock. Season with a pinch of salt. Cool and chiall the stock if you aren't intending to can it right away. The stock may be frozen or kept in the refrigerator for up to 3 days. Now to Pressure Can the Fish Stock:
Start using clean, hot jars in the preparation. Check your jars for nicks and don't use any jars that are defective for canning.

They should be clean but not sterile. If you're beginning with hot soup, start with hot jars plus hot water in the canner; if the temps are consistent, you won't lose jars to thermal shock.

Keep a supply of clean jar bands on hand. Put clean lids inside a dish and cover with boiling water; set aside until ready to use. Fill pressure canner halfway with water (usually marked on the inside.) I prefer to Add tbsp of white vinegar to this water to prevent a film from forming on my jars after they've been canned. Heat the water to the point where it will be hot when the heated jars are placed in it.

Bring fish stock to a low boil. Fill heated jars halfway with stock, allowing one inch of headspace. Apply the bands after wiping the rims and centering the hot lids on the jars. Fingertip-tighten the bands; they shouldn't be turned on too hard.

Jars at 10-pound pressure for 30 minutes (pints) or 35 minutes (quarts) - altitude adjustments may be necessary. All ow the canner to cool and restore to zero pounds pressure for itself after the timer has expired. Remove jars to a towel-lined surface and let them aside for 24 hours before checking the lids for an appropriate seal. When center is squeezed, the lids should not bend up and down. Make sure the jars are labeled.

Nutrition Calories: 2 kcal Carbohydrates: 0 g Protein: 3 g Fat: 1 g

Canned Salmon

Preparation time: 40 minutes
Cooking time: 1 hour 50 minutes
Servings: 8
Ingredients:
- 8 tbsp neutral oil
- 16 peppercorns
- Canning salt to taste
- 4 lb salmon Fillet

Directions:
Add 8 oz of salmon to that of an 8 oz canning jar, skin side down, all owing approximately 1 inch of headspace in the jar when using skin-on salmon. You can cram as much as you can into the available area.
Season with ¼ tsp salt and 2 peppercorns. Close jars with finger-tight canning lids after wiping the rims with a clean, moist cloth.
Cover pressure canner with just a tea towel or a specific rack to avoid the jars from coming into direct contact with the pot's bottom. Add two inches of water to the mix. The jars should then be placed in the pressure canner. Water should get to within 1 inch of the jars' tops. If you want to add more than one layer of jars, use a metal canning rack to separate them and add extra layers.
Follow your pressure cooker's
Directions for 110 minutes at 10 PSI (pounds per square inch). Cover 23-quart pressure canner with a lid, twist the lid to lock it, and Remove weight from the steam valve. Increase the heat to high and wait 10 minutes until the steam starts to come out in a constant stream (this removes all excess air).
After 10 minutes, gently replace 8 on the steam valve. All ow for pressure to develop up to 10 PSI as shown by the pressure gauge. Reduce heat to low and set the timer for 110 minutes after the pressure reaches 10 PSI. Continue to adjust the heat until the pressure is consistently at 10 PSI or slightly higher. To destroy any undesired microorganisms, the pressure should be maintained at 10 PSI or greater. Start the timer anew if the pressure fall s below 10 PSI at any moment.

Remove jars, then Turn heat down and let the pressure naturall y drop down. Open lid after the pressure indicator has fall en to 0, Transfer jars to a towel-lined shelf, and cool to room temperature (about 3–4 hours). When jars are cold enough to handle, push in the center of each lid and make sure it reall y doesn't pop up; if it does, the jars are securely sealed. That it is now safe to Remove lid ring, clean and dry the jars, then reinstall the ring if desired. Place items in storage. The jars may be kept at room temperature for a long time.
Nutrition Calories: 36 kcal Carbohydrates: 1 g Protein: 4 g Fat: 1 g

Fatty Fish

Preparation time: 10 minutes
Cooking time: 1 hour
Servings: 4 pints
Ingredients:
- 5 lbs Salmon/trout/mackerel/other fatty fish
- Salt to taste
- 1 cup Vinegar

Directions:
Wash fish in water with 2 tsp vinegar (2 quarts).
Remove fish's scales, fins, head, and tail, then carefully wash to remove any blood.
Cut fish into 312-inch-long pieces by splitting them lengthwise. Fill clean and hot Mason jars with one tsp of salt each, but do not Add any liquid.
Wipe jar rims with paper towels to remove any remaining fish oil. Before putting the jars in the pressure canner, adjust the lids. All ow 1 hour and 40 minutes to finish the process.
Nutrition Calories: 76 kcal Carbohydrates: 7 gProtein: 2 g Fat: 4 g

Tuna Fish

Preparation time: 10 minutes
Cooking time: 1 hour
Servings: 3 pints
Ingredients:
- 2 tbsp Oil
- Water enough to cover fish
- 4 lbs Tuna
- Salt to taste

Directions:
Once removing the viscera, carefully clean the fish and Drain residual blood.
Cut tuna in half crosswise. Bake for 4 hours at 250°F before putting the meat inside the refrigerator to firm up.
Peel skin, smudged flesh, blood vessels, fin bases, and bones from the body. Cut into quarters and pack firmly in oil or water in clean, hot Mason jars. Make sure the jars have 1 inch of headspace and that any air bubbles have been eliminated.
Set lids on the canning jars and Place se inside the pressure canner. All ow 1 hour and 20 minutes to complete the process.
Nutrition Calories: 64 kcal Carbohydrates: 1 g Protein: 3 g Fat: 5 g

Pressure Canned Whole Clams

Preparation time: 20 minutes
Cooking time: 10 minutes
Canning time: 60 minutes
Servings: 7 pints
Ingredients:
- 5 lb Clam
- 3 tbsp salt
- 2 tbsp lemon juice
- 1-gall on water

Directions:
Keep clams cold in ice until you are ready to pressure-can them.
Scrub the shells then stream them over water for 5 minutes. Open the clams and Remove meat. Save the juices.
Add gall on of water to a mixing bowl then Add t most 3 tbsp of salt. Wash clam meat in the salted water.
Add water to a shall ow saucepan then add lemon juice. Bring water to a boil. Add clam meat and boil for 2 minutes.
Heat reserved clam juices until boiling.
Drain meat and pack it loosely in the jars leaving 1-inch headspace.
Pour hot clam juice over the meat then Remove bubbles.
You may add boiling water if you run out of clam juice.
Wipe rims and Place lids and the rings on the jars. Process the jars at 10 pounds pressure for 60 minutes
Wait for pressure canner to depressurize to zero before removing the jars.
Place jars on a cooling rack for 12–24 hours undisturbed then store in a cool dry place.
Nutrition Calories: 148 kcal Total fat: 2 g carbs: 5.1 g Protein: 25.5 Sugars: 0 g Fiber: 0 g

Pressure Canned Minced Clams

Preparation time: 20 minutes
Cooking time: 10 minutes
Canning time: 60 minutes
Servings: 5 pints
Ingredients:
- 5 lb Clam
- 3 tbsp salt
- 2 tbsp lemon juice

Directions:
Keep clams cold in ice until you are ready to pressure-can them.
Scrub the shells then stream them over water for 5 minutes. Open the clams and Remove meat. Save the juices.
Add gall on of water to a mixing bowl then Add t most 3 tbsp of salt. Wash clam meat in the salted water.
Add water to a shall ow saucepan then add lemon juice. Bring water to a boil. Add clam meat and boil for 2 minutes.
Heat the reserved clam juices until boiling.
Drain meat and add it to the grinder or a food processor.
Pack ¾ cup of minced clams in a ½-pint leaving a headspace of 1 inch. Add clam juices, maintaining the headspace.
Remove any air bubbles and add more clam juice if necessary. In case you run out of clam juice, add boiling water.
Wipe rims and Place lids and the rings on the ½-pint jars. Process the jars at 10 pounds pressure for 60 minutes
Wait for pressure canner to depressurize to zero before removing the jars.
Place jars on a cooling rack undisturbed then store in a cool dry place.
Nutrition Calories: 148 kcal Total fat: 2 g Total carbs: 5.1 g Protein: 25.5 Sugars: 0 g Fiber: 0 g

Pressure Canned Shrimp

Preparation time: 20 minutes
Cooking time: 10 minutes
Canning time: 45 minutes
Servings: 10 pints
Ingredients:
- 10 lb shrimp
- ¼ cup salt
- 1 cup vinegar
- 1-gall on water

Directions:
Remove heads immediately after you catch shrimp then chill until ready to preserve them.
Wash shrimps and Drain m well.
Add gall on of water to a pot then add salt and vinegar. Boil n cook shrimp for 10 minutes.
Use a slotted spoon to Remove shrimp from the cooking liquid then rinse it in cold water and drain. Peel shrimp while packing it in the sterilized jars.
Add gall on of water with 3 tbsp of salt and bring it to a boil.
Add brine to the jars and Remove air bubbles. Add more brine if necessary.
Wipe jar rims with a cloth damped in vinegar. Place lids and the rings.
Process the jars at 10 pounds pressure for 45 minutes
Wait for pressure canner to depressurize to zero before removing the jars.
Place jars on a cooling rack undisturbed then store in a cool dry place
Nutrition Calories: 100 kcal Total fat: 2 g Total carbs: 1 g Protein: 15 g Sugars: 0 g Fiber: 0 g

Canned Oysters

Preparation time: 30 minutes
Cooking time: 10 minutes
Canning time: 75 minutes
Servings: 6 pints
Ingredients:

- 5 lb oysters
- Salt to taste Water

Directions:
Wash oysters in clean water then heat them in an oven at 400°F for 7 minutes to open.
Cool them in ice-cold water. Remove meat, placing it in water containing salt.
Drain meat and pack in the jars leaving 1-inch headspace. Add ½ tbsp of salt to each ½-pint jar and add water maintaining the headspace.
Wipe jar rims then Place lids and the rings.
Process jars at 10 pounds pressure for 75 minutes.
Wait for pressure canner to depressurize to zero before removing the jars from the canner
Place jars on a cooling rack undisturbed then store in a cool dry place
Nutrition Calories: 68 kcal Total fat: 3 g Total carbs: 0 g Protein: 7 Sugars: 0 g Fiber: 0 g Sodium: 87 mg Potassium: 0 mg

River Fish

Preparation time: 20 minutes
Canning time: 1 hour and 45 minutes
Servings: 4 pints
Ingredients:
- 1 trout
- 1 tsp salt

Directions:
Process trout by cutting off the heads, tails, and fins. Discard those. Pack jars with fish, leaving 1-inch headspace, then add ½ tbsp of salt into each jar.
Process jars at 11 pounds pressure for 1 hour and 45 minutes.
Let cool before removal and storage.
Nutrition Calories: 190 kcal Total fat: 8.36 g Potassium: 510 mg Sodium: 69 mg Protein: 26.89 g

Shad

Preparation time: 20 minutes
Canning time: 1 hour and 40 minutes
Servings: 4 pints
Ingredients:
- 1 shad
- 1 tsp salt
- 2 cups water

Directions:
Make brine by dissolving 1 cup of salt in 1 gallon of water.
Cut fish into jar-length pieces. Let soak for 1 hour, then drain for 10 minutes.
Pack the fish into jars, leaving 1-inch headspace. Process the jars at 10 pounds pressure for 1 hour and 40 minutes.
Let cool for 12 hours before removal and storage.
Nutrition: Calories:362 kcal Cholesterol: 138 mg Sodium: 93.6 mg Potassium: 708.5 mg Total carbs: 0 g Protein: 31.3 g

Easy Tomato Crab Soup

Preparation time: 10 minutes
Cooking time: 25 minutes
Servings: 4
Ingredients:
- 2 tbsp olive oil
- 2 garlic cloves, minced
- ¼ cup chopped onion
- 1 (10.75-oz) can of condensed tomato soup
- 1 (14.5-oz) can diced tomatoes
- 1 (6-oz) can crabmeat
- 1-pint half-and-half cream

Directions:
Cook garlic and onion in oil until softened. Stir in tomato soup, tomatoes, and crabmeat and heat through. Stir in half-and-half and cook until bubbly.
Nutrition Calories: 242 kcal Total fat: 16.4 g Cholesterol: 59 mg Sodium: 520 mg Total carbohydrates: 14 g Protein: 10.1 g

Gina's Crab Stuffed Chicken Breast

Preparation time: 10 minutes
Cooking time: 1 hour and 30 minutes
Servings: 3
Ingredients:
- ¼ cup butter
- ¼ cup all-purpose flour
- ¾ cup chicken broth
- ¾ cup milk
- ⅓ cup dry white wine
- ¼ cup onion, chopped
- 1 cup buttery round crackers, crushed
- 1 (8-oz) can crabmeat
- 2 tbsp chopped fresh parsley
- 4 skinless, boneless chicken breast halves
- 1 cup shredded Cheddar cheese

Directions:
To make sauce: melt butter. Stir in flour until smooth. Cook and stir for 5 minutes, then gradually stir in broth, milk, and white wine. Cook on low until the sauce thickens fully, about 20 minutes. Remove from heat and set aside.
Mix onion, cracker crumbs, crabmeat, parsley, and ¼ cup of the sauce.
Pound chicken breasts to ¼-inch thickness. Spoon ¼ of the crab mixture on the edge of each chicken breast; roll up. Place chicken rolls in a lightly greased 9x13-inch baking dish, fold side down, then top with the remaining white sauce.
Cover dish and bake at 350°F (175°C) or until the chicken juices run clear about 1 hour. Sprinkle with cheese and bake, uncovered, until the cheese is lightly browned, about 5 minutes more.
Nutrition Calories: 797 kcal Total fat: 43.4 g Cholesterol: 188 mg Sodium: 1221 mg Total carbohydrates: 43.4 g Protein: 51.6 g

Hot Crabmeat Dip

Preparation time: 10 minutes
Cooking time: 45 minutes
Servings: 3
Ingredients:
- 1 (8-oz) package cream cheese, softened
- 1 tbsp milk
- 2 tbsp minced onion
- 1 tsp prepared horseradish
- ¼ tsp salt
- 1 pinch ground black pepper
- 1 (6-oz) can crabmeat, drained and flaked
- ⅓ cup sliced almonds

Directions:
Preheat oven to 300°F (150°C).
mix the cream cheese, milk, onion, horseradish, salt, pepper, and crabmeat. Spread mixture into a pie pan or shall ow baking dish. Sprinkle almonds over the crabmeat mixture.
Bake in preheated oven for 45 minutes, or until bubbly and lightly browned.
Nutrition Calories: 78 kcal Total fat: 6.6 g Cholesterol: 25 mg Sodium: 114 mg Total carbohydrates: 1.2 g Protein: 3.9 g

Janet's Appetizer

Preparation time: 10 minutes
Cooking time: 5 minutes
Servings: 5
Ingredients:
- 1 cup mayonnaise
- 1 cup minced red onion
- 1 cup shredded white Cheddar cheese
- 1 cup crab meat (optional)
- 1 tsp Dijon-style prepared mustard
- ½ tsp garlic powder
- ½ (1 lb) loaf sliced pumpernickel party bread
- Lemon pepper to taste

Directions:
Preheat your oven's broiler.
stir mayonnaise, onion, cheddar, crabmeat, mustard, and garlic powder.
Arrange bread slices on a cookie sheet. Place 1 tbsp of the mixture on each slice. Sprinkle the bread slice liberally with lemon pepper spice (this is the key ingredient, so don't be shy with the spice!). Broil for less than 2 minutes.
Nutrition Calories: 357 Total fat: 27.6 g Cholesterol: 40 mg Sodium: 488 mg Total carbohydrates: 17.4 g Protein: 10.4 g

Fish Rice Casserole

Preparation time: 10 – 20 minutes
Cooking time: 30 Minutes
Servings: 4
Ingredients:
- 14 oz. fish
- 2 cups cooked rice, divided
- 1 egg
- ¼ cup milk
- ¼ tsp. salt
- ¼ tsp. pepper
- 2 tbsps. Butter

Directions::
Grease 8-inch baking dish.
Preheat oven to 375°F.
Drain fish, saving the juice to use later.
Spread 1 cup of the rice in the baking dish.
Spread fish over the rice, flaking it finely.
Pour reserved fish juice over the fish.
Spread remaining 1 cup of rice over the top.
mix the egg, milk, salt, and pepper.
Transfer egg mixture evenly over the casserole.
Dot with butter.
Bake until heated through and golden, about 30 minutes.
Fill jars with fish and rice casserole.
Put jars in canner and Fill with water to the jar rings.
Close and lock pressure canner and Boil then add cooking weight to the top.
After 20 minutes, turn heat to medium and cook for 75 minutes.
Turn off heat and leave canner alone until it has cooled completely to room temperature.
After canner has cooled, remove jars from the canner and check for sealing.
Nutrition: Cholesterol 0mg Calories: 209.6 Fat: 5.0g Carbs: 18.8g Protein: 21.1g Sugar 0 g

Pasta

Garlic Oyster Linguini

Preparation time: 10 minutes
Cooking time: 10 minutes
Servings: 4
Ingredients:
- ¼ cup butter
- 8 oz fresh mushrooms, quartered
- 1 tsp Cajun seasoning
- 1 tsp minced garlic
- 24 shucked oysters, quartered
- ½ cup whole corn kernels, blanched
- ⅔ cup French-style green beans, chopped
- 2 tbsp chopped pimento peppers
- ½ cup seafood stock
- 10 oz fresh linguine pasta
- 2 tbsp butter
- 2 tbsp all -purpose flour
- 2 tbsp chopped fresh parsley
- 3 tbsp thinly sliced green onion
- 4 oz crabmeat

Directions:
melt 2 tbsp of butter or margarine. Stir in flour to make a paste. Set roux aside.
Sauté onions, mushrooms, Cajun spice, and garlic in ¼ cup of butter or margarine over medium-high heat for 2 minutes. Add oysters, corn, string beans, and pimento. Sauté for 1 ½ minute. Add stock and linguine, and bring to a slight simmer.
Fold in roux until the sauce thickens, then Reduce heat . Fold in parsley and scall ions. Fold in lump crabmeat, and heat through. Serve immediately.
Nutrition Calories: 497 Total fat: 20.7 g Cholesterol: 146 mg Sodium: 577 mg Total carbohydrates: 51.1 g Protein: 27 g

Vegetable Soup

Preparation time: 15 minutes
Cooking time: 30 minutes
Servings: 6
Ingredients:
- 1/3 cup dried vegetable flakes (any combination of tomatoes, peas, onions, broccoli, zucchini, celery, carrots)
- ¼ teaspoon dried parsley
- ¼ teaspoon dried sweet basil
- Pinch garlic powder
- Pinch onion powder
- 1 tablespoon bulgar wheat
- 1 teaspoon pasta, broken if large pieces
- 2 cups chicken or beef

Directions::
Place vegetable flakes, parsley, basil, garlic powder, onion powder, bulgar wheat, and pasta in a pint thermos. Bring broth or stock to a rolling boil and pour over dry Ingredients. Cover thermos and close securely for 10-15 minutes. Add salt and pepper to taste.
Nutrition: Cholesterol 0mg Calories: Fat: 2.3g Protein: 6.9g Carbs: 32.3g Sugar 0 g

Lean Turkey Lasagna

Preparation time: 10 – 20 minutes
Cooking time: 40 Minutes
Servings: 8
Ingredients:
- 1¼ lbs. ground lean turkey
- 2 cloves garlic, minced
- 1 tbsp. olive oil
- 4 sheets no-boil lasagna noodles
- Fresh basil leaves
- ½ cup parmesan Tomato sauce
- 1 tbsp. minced olive oil
- 2 minced cloves garlic
- 6 oz. tomato paste
- 3 tbsps. Chopped basil
- 2 tbsps. Shredded parmesan
- ¼ tsp. salt Cheese Filling
- 5 oz. container part-skim ricotta
- 1/3 cup shredded parmesan cheese
- ½ cup low-fat mozzarella
- 1 egg

Directions::
Preheat oven to 350°F. Prepare eight 6-ounce canning jars on a baking sheet.
In a sizable skillet, heat olive oil over medium heat. Fry ground turkey with garlic until the meat is browned and cooked through. Transfer to a large bowl and set it aside.
Heat olive oil in a medium saucepan over medium heat. Fry garlic until fragrant, about 40 seconds. Pour in the diced tomatoes, tomato paste, basil, parmesan, and salt, and Bring liquid to a boil. Simmer for about 10 minutes while covered.
Pour thickened tomato sauce together with the turkey and mix thoroughly.
mix together the cheese Filling ingredients until well-combined. To assemble, line the bottom of the jars with 2 tbsps.

Of the turkey mixture, then cover with noodle pieces, cheese Filling, and a basil leaf. Repeat the layers once more until the jar is full. Finish off with a generous sprinkle of parmesan.

Cover jars with aluminum foil to prevent the cheese from burning too quickly. Bake the jars for 35 minutes before removing the foil, and then bake it uncovered for another 10 minutes.

Best served warm.

Nutrition: Cholesterol 0mg Calories: 377 Fat: 20g Carbs: 621g Protein: 30g Sugar 0 g

Chicken Noodle Soup

Preparation time: 10 minutes
Cooking time: 25 minutes
Servings: 4
Ingredients:
- ¼ cup red lentils
- 1 bay leaf
- 1 cup egg noodles
- 1/8 tsp. celery seed
- 1/8 tsp. garlic powder
- ½ tsp. dial seed
- 1 ½ tbsp. chicken bouillon granules
- 2 tbsp. dehydrated sliced onion
- 8 cups water

Directions::
Add all ingredients except water into the glass jar. Seal jar with lid tightly and shake well.
To cook: Add water and jar content to the saucepan and bring to boil.
Reduce heat and simmer for 25 minutes.
Serve and enjoy.
Nutrition: Cholesterol 0mg Calories: 108 Fat: 1.1g Protein: 5.2g Carbs: 19.6g Sugar 0 g

JAM
Plum and Orange Jam

Preparation time: 30 minutes
Cooking time: 5 minutes
Serving: 10 ½ pt.
Ingredients:

- 10 c. plums
- 1 c. orange juice
- 1 package of pectin
- 3 c. sugar
- 3 tbsp. orange zest (grated)
- 1 ½ tsp. cinnamon powder

Directions::
Take 10 cups of plums and Remove skin by peeling. Finely Chop se plums and Add to the medium-sized pots. Now take one cup of orange juice and pour over the plums.
Wait for juice and plums mixture to boil.
When it starts boiling, lower the heat. Let this mixture simmer for 5 to 7 minutes. Meanwhile, Keep pot covered while it is simmering. When the plums have become soft, open the packet of pectin and add to the plum mixture.
Turn on flame again and stir once or twice. When it starts boiling, stir continuously.
Now add sugar, cinnamon, and orange zest. Keep orange zest grated so that you can add it quickly.
Wait for it to boil again while stirring; otherwise, sugar will stick to the pot. When the sugar has dissolved completely, Keep mixture boiling for one minute.
Then Take mixture off of the stove. Before adding the mixture to the jar, Remove foam from the surface of the mixture by skimming.
Heat jars to sterilize them and Pour mixture while still hot.
Clean rims of the jar, leave adequate headspace, tap the jar to release the trapped air.

Get canner ready with boiling water and Place jars correctly inside it. Process jars in this canner for 5 minutes. After 5 minutes, Take jars out of the canner gnd Place m somewhere cold. All ow their temperature to get down and store them later after checking the seal.
Nutrition: Calories: 50; Carbohydrates: 13 g; Fats: 0 g; Protein: 0

Kiwi Jam

Preparation time: 15 minutes
Cooking time: 40 minutes
Canning time: 10 minutes
Total time: 1 hour
Servings: 40
Ingredients:
- 1½ cups kiwis, peeled and mashed
- 1½ apples, halved
- 1/3 cup pineapple juice
- 2 tablespoons fresh lemon juice
- 2 cups white sugar

Directions::
Cook mashed kiwi, apples, pineapple juice, and lemon juice until boiling.
Add sugar and stir to dissolve.
Now set the heat to low and cook for about 30 minutes.
In 5 (½-pint) hot sterilized jars, divide the jam, .
Slide knife around the insides of each jar to remove air bubbles. 6.
Close each jar with a lid and screw on the ring.
Arrange jars in a boiling water canner and process for about 10 minutes.
Remove jars from water canner and place on wood surface
Cool then, press the top jar's lid to ensure that the seal is tight.
The canned jam can be preserved in the pantry for up to 1 year.
Nutrition: Calories 47 Total Fat 0.1 g Saturated Fat 0 g Cholesterol 0 mg Sodium 0 mg Fiber 0.44 g Sugar 11.7 g Protein 0.1 g

Strawberry Jam

Preparation time: 20 minutes
Cooking time: 15 minutes
Serving: 5 c.
Ingredients:
- 2 lb. hauled strawberries
- 4 c. white sugar
- ¼ c. lemon juice

Directions::
Clean all strawberries and crush them all unless they make 4 cups.
Take a saucepan and put mashed strawberries, lemon juice, and sugar in it.
Mix all these ingredients thoroughly.
Keep mixture stirring until the granules of sugar are dissolved.
Wait for mixture to boil and keep stirring.
When the temperature reaches 220 F, turn off the stove.
Pour mixture into the jars and secure the lids.
Put them in the water bath and let them process for 15 minutes.
Nutrition : Calories : 40; Carbohydrates: 11g; Fats: 0 g; Protein: 0g.

Blueberry and Lime Jam

Preparation time: 30 minutes
Cooking time: 10 minutes
Servings: 6 pints
Ingredients:
- 4 ½ cups blueberries
- 5 cups sugar
- 1 package dry pectin
- 1 tbsp lime zest
- ⅓ cup lime juice

Directions::
crush blueberries 1 layer at a time, combining with pectin.
Boil over high heat, stirring regularly, and then whisk in the sugar until it dissolves.
Return to a rolling boil with the grated lime peel and lime juice.
Remove from the heat and transfer to jars.
Place jars in a warm water bath for 15 minutes.
All ow cooling fully before storing in an airtight container.
Nutrition Calories: 6 kcal Carbohydrates: 1 g Protein: 0g Fat: 0g

Apricot Jam

Preparation time: 15 minutes
Cooking time: 45 minutes
Servings: 10 cups
Ingredients:
- 8 cups diced apricots, cored and peeled
- ¼ cup lemon juice
- 6 cups sugar

Directions::
combine all ingredients and whisk until the sugar is dissolved.
Once mixture has reached a rolling boil, cook for 30 minutes, then remove from the heat and pour into jars.
Place jars in a water bath for 10 minutes.
Remove from the oven and set aside to cool fully before storing.
Nutrition Calories: 65 kcal Carbohydrates: 9 g Protein: 1 g Fat: 2 g

Mango Jam

Preparation time: 30 minutes
Cooking time: 15 minutes
Servings: 8 cups
Ingredients:
- 4 cups diced mangoes
- ½ cup water
- 2 tbsp lemon juice
- 3 tbsp powdered pectin
- 7 cups sugar

Directions::
Mango flesh should be washed, peeled, and diced. Combine chopped mango, water, and lemon juice in a large, heavy-bottomed saucepan. Cover and cook until the fruit is tender. Puree for a smooth jam, and mash for a thick jam.
Fill jars halfway with the water and Boil for 10 minutes. Turn off heat and Keep jars in the hot water until you're ready to Fill them.
Pectin should be whisked into the mango puree. Boil (as high as possible), then immediately Add sugar. Bring to a rapid boil (do not stir or the mixture will froth) and cook for 1 minute. Turn heat off and skim the froth.
In a dish of boiling water, Place lids. When you're ready to use the lids, take them out of the water and lay them on the jars to Seal m. Fill heated jars halfway with jam, all owing a ¼-inch (0.5cm) headspace. Remove any bubbles, double-Check headspace, then clean the rims with a moist paper towel and seal.
Process for 10 minutes in a boiling water bath canner (time start once the water returns to a full boil). When the timer goes off, Turn off heat and let the jars sit in the water for 5 minutes before putting them on a towel-covered bench to cool overnight.
Nutrition Calories: 215 kcal Carbohydrates: 7 g Protein: 1g Fat: 0.2 g

Blueberry Jam

Preparation time: 20 minutes
Cooking time: 30 minutes
Servings: 6 ½-pint jars
Ingredients:
- 2 pints blueberries
- 2 tbsp lemon juice
- 3 oz pectin
- 5 ¼ cups sugar

Directions::
combine all ingredients and Boil, constantly stirring until the sugar has dissolved approximately 20 minutes.
Remove from heat and pour into jars.
Cool for 30 minutes in a water bath. Let aside to cool fully before storing.
Nutrition Calories: 65 kcal Carbohydrates: 9 g Protein: 1 g Fat: 2 g

Apple Sauce

Preparation time: 60 minutes
Cooking time: 20 minutes
Servings: 1 quart
Ingredients:
- 3 lb cooking apples like Cortland, McIntosh, Bramley
- 2 tbsp white sugar (optional)
- 2 tsp ground cinnamon (optional)
- Water

Directions::
Peel, core, and quarter the apples, then Place in a big saucepan and simmer until they are tender.
Puree the apples in a food processor, then return mixture to the pan and heat to a boil. If desired, sprinkle with sugar or cinnamon. While boiling, pour into jars.
Place jars in a water bath for approximately 20 minutes.
Set aside to cool fully before storing.
Nutrition Calories: 68 kcal Carbohydrates: 7 g Protein: 2 g Fat: 3 g

Basil Strawberry Jam

Preparation time: 10 minutes
Cooking time: 45 minutes
Servings: 10
Ingredients:
- 7 cups sugar
- 1 pack of 1 ¾ oz powdered fruit pectin
- 12 cups fresh strawberries
- ½ tsp butter
- ⅓ cup fresh basil snipped

Directions::
To prepare the jam, Combine berries in a heavy boiling saucepan.
Gently smash berries and combine with the butter and pectin in a mixing bowl.
Reduce heat to medium and wait a few minutes for the mixture to heat up.
Add sugar and continue to beat until it is fully dissolved.
Take it from the heat and use a spoon to scrape away the froth.
Stir the clipped basil into the jam mixture well.
After that, Take pre-sterilized jars and Fill them with the strawberry basil jam mixture.
Leave a ½-inch gap at the top.
Clean jar rims with a moist cloth before closing them with the lid and band.
Fill tanning kettle halfway with water and set the jars in it.
Set canning timer for 5–7 minutes and modify the duration according to your altitude.
Remove hot jars from the canning process, Wipe m down, and Remove bands.
Keep jam in a dry, cold location and enjoy it.
Nutrition Calories: 69 kcal Carbohydrates: 11 g Protein: 2 g Fat: 1 g

Spiked Peach Jam with Ginger

Preparation time: 30 minutes
Cooking time: 25 minutes
Servings: 5 ½-pint jars
Ingredients:
- 4 ½ cups peeled peaches finely chopped
- 4 tbsp lemon juice
- 3 cups white sugar
- 1 tsp ground ginger
- 1 (1.75 oz) package of light pectin
- ⅓ cup Amaretto liqueur

Directions::
To keep peaches from browning, Place in a glass or plastic box with a cover and add lemon juice right away. Combine sugar and ginger in a mixing bowl. Cover and marinate for 8 hours to overnight in a cool location.
Examine 5 ½-pint jars for fractures and corrosion on the rings, and eliminate any that are unsatisfactory. Place in a pot of simmering water until the jam is ready. In warm soapy water, wash fresh, unused lids and rings.
Transfer peaches, as well as any remaining liquid to a big saucepan. Stir in the pectin and gently Bring mixture to a full rolling boil, stirring constantly. Cook for 1 minute while continually stirring. Remove from heat and mix in the amaretto liqueur, tasting as you go.
Fill the prepared jars with peach jam to within ¼ inch of the top. To eliminate any air bubbles, run a knife or thin spatula along the insides of the jars.
To remove any spillage, Wipe rims with a wet paper towel.
Cover with lids and secure with rings.
Fill a big stockpot partly with water and place a rack in the bottom. Boil, then use a holder to drop jars 2 inches apart into the hot water. More boiling water should be added to Cover jars by at least 1 inch. Boil, then reduce to a simmer for 10 minutes.
Take jars from the stockpot and arrange them several inches apart on a cloth-covered or wood surface.

All ow yourself a 24-hour rest period without moving. To guarantee that the lids do not slide up or down, gently push the center of each lid with your finger.
Remove rings and Keep in a cold, dark location.
Nutrition Calories: 70.1 kcal Carbohydrates: 1 g Protein: 0.2 g Fat: 0.1 g

Savory Peach Jam Preserve

Preparation time: 10 minutes
Cooking time: 25–30 minutes
Servings: 8
Ingredients:
- 10 cups peaches chopped
- 5 cups sugar
- 3 tsp lemon juice

Directions::
To begin, grab your glass bowl and Add peaches, sugar, and lemon juice one by one.
Gently Combine ingredients. All ow approximately 60–70 minutes for the peaches to soak up the sugar.
Pour peach mixture into a saucepan and cook over medium heat.
All ow the peach mixture to simmer for approximately 5 minutes.
Increase the heat to high, stir gently, and cook for approximately 20 minutes, or until the sugar has fully melted.
Remove it from the fire after that. Do not Pour hot preserves straight into the jars. All ow 15–20 minutes for cooling.
Finally, gently Fill the pre-sterilized jars.
Seal jars' tops with waxed discs, then cover them with elastic bands and cellophane or lids.
All ow jars to cool completely before labeling them. Store in a cool, dry location.
Nutrition Calories: 65 kcal Carbohydrates: 9 g Protein: 1 g Fat: 2 g

Pineapple & Maraschino Cherry Jam

Preparation time: 10 minutes
Cooking time: 15 minutes
Servings: 7
Ingredients:
- 1 orange, large size
- 3 cups chopped pears cored
- ¾ cup pineapple, crushed and drained
- 5 cups sugar
- ¼ cup Maraschino cherries chopped
- ¼ cup lemon juice
- 1 pack of 3 oz powdered pectin

Directions:
Begin by peeling the orange and chopping the pulp.
To prepare jam, Combine pineapple, pears, lemon juice, pectin, cherries, and pulp in a saucepan.
Keep heat on high and wait a few minutes for the mixture to heat up.
Finally, whisk in sugar and let it dissolve fully.
Remove it from the heat and use a spoon to Remove froth.
Fill jars with the fruity jam mixture and set them in the pre-sterilized jars.
Keep jam in a dry, cold place and enjoy it.
Nutrition Calories: 69 kcal Carbohydrates: 11 g Protein: 2 g Fat: 1 g

Triple Berry Spiced Jam

Preparation time: 30 minutes
Cooking time: 25 minutes
Servings: 10 ½-pints
Ingredients:
- 6 cups sugar
- 4 cups crushed strawberries
- 2 cups crushed blueberries
- 2 cups crushed raspberries
- 2 tbsp shredded lemon peel
- ½ cup lemon juice
- 1 tsp ground cinnamon

Directions::
Combine sugar, blueberries, crushed strawberries, raspberries, lemon juice and lemon peel in a 6–8-quart heavy saucepan. Over medium heat, Boil, constantly stirring to dissolve the sugar. Cook, stirring regularly, for 25–30 minutes, uncovered until the mixture sheets off a metal spoon. Stir in the cinnamon until it's well blended.
Fill ½-pint canning jars halfway with hot jam, leaving ¼-inch headspace. Adjust lids and screw bands after wiping jar rims.
In a boiling-water canner, process Filled jars for 10 minutes (when water returns to boiling).
Remove jars from the canner and Place m on wire racks to cool. This recipe makes 10 ½-pints.
Nutrition Calories: 3 kcal Carbohydrates: 1 g Protein: 0 g Fat: 0 g

Apricot Lavender Jam

Preparation time: 30 minutes
Cooking time: 5 minutes
Servings: 8 ½-pint jars
Ingredients:
- 4 ½ cups white sugar
- 1 tbsp dried lavender blossoms
- 3 ½ lb fresh apricots, sliced and pitted
- 2 tbsp lemon juice
- (1 ¾ oz) package fruit pectin (Pectin Light no sugar)

Directions::
combine ½ cup of sugar and lavender flowers; pulse tiall the lavender blossoms are finely diced, and the sugar is aromatic. Measure apricots; you should have around 5 cups of ready-to-eat fruit. Place in a plastic or glass jar with a tight-fitting cover and chop coarsely. Combine lavender sugar and lemon juice in a mixing bowl. Refrigerate overnight, covered.
Inspect 8 ½-pint jars for fractures and corrosion on the rings, and reject any that are unsatisfactory. Place in a pot of simmering water until the jam is ready. In warm soapy water, wash fresh, unused lids and rings.
In a dish, combine ¼ cup of the leftover sugar and pectin; pour over apricots. Mix the fruit mixture well in a big pot. Bring to a high rolling boil, occasionally stirring, until it stops bubbling. To thoroughly dissolve the sugar, Add rest sugar and stir well, scraping the bottom of the pan. Cook for 1 minute while continually stirring.
Pour apricot jam into the prepared jars as soon as possible, Filling them to within ¼ inch of the surface. To eliminate any air bubbles, run a good knife or thin spatula along the insides of the jars. To remove any spillage, Wipe rims with a wet paper towel. Cover with lids and secure with rings.
Fill a big stockpot partly with water and place a rack in the bottom. Boil, then use a holder to drop jars 2 inches apart into the hot water. More boiling water should be added to Cover jars by at least 1 inch. Boil, then reduce to a simmer for 10 minutes.

Take jars from the stockpot and arrange them several inches apart on a cloth-covered or wood surface. All ow for a 24-hour rest period without moving the jars. To guarantee that the lids do not slide up or down, gently push the center of each lid with your finger.
Remove rings and Keep m in a cold, dark location.
Nutrition Calories: 3 kcal Carbohydrates: 8.4 g Protein: 0.2 g Fat: 0 g

Balsamic Vinegar Ruby Port Jelly

Preparation time: 30 minutes
Cooking time: 10 minutes
Servings: 4 ½-pints
Ingredients:
- ⅓ cup balsamic vinegar
- ¼ cup coarsely orange peel shredded
- 3 cups sugar
- 2 cups ruby port
- ½ of a 6-oz package of liquid fruit pectin

Directions::
Combine orange peel and vinegar in a small saucepan. Boil, then Turn off heat. Cover and cook for 3–5 minutes, or until the vinegar has been reduced to ¼ cup.
Remove pan from the heat. Cover and set aside to cool. Using a fine- mesh screen, strain the mixture; discard the peel.
Combine sugar, reduced vinegar, and port in a 4–6-quart heavy saucepan. Over high heat, bring to a full rolling boil, stirring frequently. Stir in the pectin quickly.
Return to a high rolling boil, continually stirring. Cook for 1 minute on high heat, stirring regularly. Remove pan from the heat. With a metal spoon, quickly skim off the froth.
Fill ½-pint canning jars halfway with heated Jelly, leaving ¼-inch headspace. Adjust lids and screw bands after wiping jar rims.
Place jars in a water bath for 10 minutes.
Remove jars from the canner and Place m on wire racks to cool. This recipe makes 4 ½-pints.
Nutrition Calories: 5 kcal Carbohydrates: 1 g Protein: 0.2 g Fat: 0.1 g

Cayenne Tomato Jam

Preparation time: 20 minutes
Cooking time: 30 hours
Servings: 4 cups
Ingredients:
- 4 lb tomatoes, peeled and chopped
- 1 apple, peeled and chopped
- 1 cup raw sugar
- 1 diced yellow onion
- ½ cup brown sugar
- ¼ cup apple cider vinegar
- 3 tbsp lemon juice
- 1 tsp salt
- ½ tsp ground cayenne pepper

Directions::
Bring apple, tomatoes, sugar, brown sugar, onion, lemon juice, apple cider vinegar, salt, and cayenne to a boil. Reduce heat to low and cook, stirring periodically, for approximately 2 hours 30 minutes, or until black and syrupy.
Continue to boil for another 30 minutes or until the mixture thickens to a jam-like consistency. Remove jam from the heat and set aside to cool for 1–2 hours. Refrigerate after transferring to closed containers.
Nutrition Calories: 5 kcal Carbohydrates: 12.9 g Protein: 0.6 g Fat: 0.1 g

Mixed Berry Agave Jam

Preparation time: 12 minutes
Cooking time: 40 minutes
Servings: 4 ½-pint jars
Ingredients:
- 4 cups crushed mixed berries
- 3 tbsp Ball Real Fruit
- ½ tbsp bottled lemon juice
- ¾ cup agave syrup

Directions::
Prepare a water canner by Filling it halfway with boiling water. Heat jars in a saucepan of simmering water tiall ready to use, but not Boil m. Set aside with bands after washing lids in warm soapy water.
Combine crushed berries and lemon juice. Sprinkle pectin evenly over berries and cook over high heat, stirring regularly, until the mixture reaches a full rolling boil that cannot be stirred down.
Add agave syrup and whisk to combine. Bring mixture back to a full boil. 1 minute of vigorous boiling, stirring continually. Remove pan from the heat. If necessary, skim the froth.
Fill a heated jar halfway with hot jam, leaving a 14-inch headspace. Air bubbles should be removed. Wipe jar's rim. Apply band to the jar's center and adjust it to fingertip tightness. In a boiling water canner, Place jar. Repeat until all of the jars are full.
Adjust for altitude and process jars for 10 minutes. Remove jars from heat, remove lids, and set aside for 5 minutes. Remove jars and set them aside to cool for 12–24 hours. When the center of the lid is squeezed, it should not bend.
Nutrition: Calories: 1 kcal Carbohydrates: 4 g Protein: 0 g Fat: 0 g

Strawberry-Rhubarb Jam

Preparation time: 30 minutes
Cooking time: 10 minutes
Servings: 12 ½-pint jars
Ingredients:
- 4 ¼ cups diced rhubarb
- 4 ¼ cups sliced fresh strawberries
- 2 tbsp lemon juice
- 2 (1 ¾ oz) packages powdered fruit pectin
- ½ tsp butter (optional)
- 10 cups white sugar
- 12 ½-pint canning jars with lids and rings

Directions::
Combine rhubarb, strawberries, lemon juice, fruit pectin, and butter. (Butter is optional, but it helps prevent the jam from foaming up.) Stir the fruit combination to assist the juice in developing, then gradually Add sugar, approximately 1 cup at a time, until the sugar dissolves and the juice begins to boil. Increase heat to medium-high, bringing the mixture to a full rolling boil, then cook for 1 minute while stirring constantly. Any foam that develops should be skimmed off.
Boil jars and lids for at least 5 minutes to sterilize them. Fill the hot, sterilized jars to ¼ inch of the top with the jam using a Jelly funnel and a soup ladle. To eliminate any air bubbles, run a knife or a small spatula along the insides of the jars after they've been Filled. To eliminate any food residue, Wipe jar rims with a wet paper towel. Screw on the rings and cover with lids.
Fill a big stockpot partly with water and place a rack in the bottom. Boil at high heat, then use a holder to gently drop the jars into the saucepan. All ow for a 2-inch gap between the jars. If required, Additional boiling water till the water level is at least one inch over the jars' tops. Bring water to a rolling boil, then cover and cook for 5 minutes.
Remove jars from the stockpot and set them several inches apart on a cloth-covered or wood surface to cool. Do not touch or move the jars until they have cooled to help the jam set.

Once cool, squeeze the top of each lid with your finger to ensure a firm seal (the lid doesn't move up and down at all). Keep it in a cool, dark place.
Nutrition Calories: 4 kcal Carbohydrates: 10.8 g Protein: 0.6 gFat: 0.2 g

Nectarine-Mango Jam

Preparation time: 40 minutes
Cooking time: 5 minutes
Servings: 7 ½-pints
Ingredients:
- 2 cups finely chopped nectarines
- ¼ cup lemon juice
- 7 ½ cups sugar
- 2 cups chopped peeled mangoes
- ½ of a 6-oz package of liquid fruit pectin

Directions::
Mix nectarines and lemon juice in a 6–8-quart saucepan. Crush nectarines using a potato masher. Combine sugar and mangoes in a mixing bowl.
Boil, constantly stirring to dissolve the sugar. Stir in the pectin quickly. Bring to a high rolling boil, continually stirring. Cook for 1 minute on high heat, stirring regularly. Remove pan from the heat and use a metal spoon to rapidly skim off the froth.
Fill ½-pint canning jars halfway with hot jam, leaving ¼-inch headspace. Adjust lids and screw bands after wiping jar rims.
In a boiling-water canner, process full jars for 5 minutes (time starts when water returns to boiling). Remove jars from the canner and cool on wire racks for 20 minutes, twisting and tilting jars to spread fruit evenly within the jam. As needed, repeat the process.
Nutrition Calories: 6 kcal Carbohydrates: 1 g Protein: 0 g Fat: 0 g

Tomato-Basil Jam

Preparation time: 30 minutes
Cooking time: 11 minutes
Servings: 5 ½-pints
Ingredients:
- ½ lb ripe tomatoes, peeled
- ¼ cup lemon juice
- 3 tbsp snipped fresh basil
- 3 cups sugar
- 1 1 ¾-oz package powdered fruit pectin

Directions::
Tomatoes should be seeded, cored, and coarsely chopped. In a 6–8-. quart enamel, stainless-steel, or non-stick heavy saucepan, measure 3 ½ cups of chopped tomatoes. Boil, stirring periodically, then
Turn off heat. Cover and cook for 10 minutes. Return 3 ⅓ cups of tomatoes to the saucepan. Combine lemon juice and basil in a mixing bowl.
Combine ¼ cup sugar and pectin in a small dish; add to tomato mixture. Bring to a high rolling boil, continually stirring. Add remaining 2 ¾ cups of sugar and mix well. Return to a high rolling boil, continually stirring. Cook for 1 minute on high heat, stirring regularly. Remove pan from the heat and use a metal spoon to rapidly skim off the froth.
Fill ½-pint canning jars halfway with hot jam, leaving ¼-inch headspace. Adjust lids and screw bands after wiping jar rims.
In a boiling-water canner, process full jars for 5 minutes (time starts when water returns to boiling). Remove jars from the canner and Place m on wire racks to cool. This recipe makes 5 ½-pints.
Nutrition Calories: 3 kcal Carbohydrates: 1 g Protein: 1 g Fat: 0.1 g

Strawberry Freezer Jam

Preparation time: 30 minutes
Cooking time: 30 minutes
Servings: 5 ½-pints
Ingredients:
- 8 cups strawberries
- ⅔ cups sugar
- 5 tbsp instant powdered fruit pectin
- 1 tbsp shredded lemon peel

Directions::
Mash 1 cup of strawberries Continue crushing and adding berries until you have a total of 4 cups of crushed berries. Combine sugar and pectin in a large mixing dish. Combine 4 cups of smashed strawberries and the lemon peel in a mixing bowl. 3 minutes of stirring
Fill ½-pint freezer containers halfway with jam, leaving ½-inch headroom. Seal and label the container.
All ow 30 minutes for the mixture to come to room temperature. Freeze for up to a year in the freezer.
Nutrition Calories: 2 kcal Carbohydrates: 6 g Protein: 0 g Fat: 0 g

Raspberry Peach Jam

Preparation time: 35 minutes
Cooking time: 20 minutes
Canning time: 12 minutes
Servings: 2 ½-pint jars
Ingredients:
- 2 cups chopped peaches
- 2 tsp lemon juice
- 4 cups raspberries
- 7 cups sugar

Directions::
Mix all ingredients in a medium mixing bowl. In the meantime, boil some water in a boiling-water canner.
Transfer to a saucepan and put inside an oven.
Cook over low heat for 16 minutes, stirring occasionally until the mixture becomes bubbly.
Remove from oven and carefully scoop off the foam.
Carefully pour in 2 250ml hot jars ensuring you leave ¼-inch to the brim. Scoop bubbles if any.
Tightly Close lid and immerse the jar in the boiling-water canner for 12 minutes.
Once the 12 minutes elapses, Remove jar from the boiling water and leave it to cool.
Enjoy!
Nutrition Calories 66 kcal Saturated fat: 0 g Cholesterol: 0 mg Sodium: 0 mg Carbohydrate: 16 g Fiber: 0 g Protein: 0 g

Tri-Berry Jam

Preparation time: 20 minutes
Cooking time: 10 minutes
Canning time: 10 minutes
Servings: 10 ½-pint jars
Ingredients:
- 3 cups fresh or frozen red raspberries
- 3 cups fresh or frozen strawberries
- ½ cups fresh or frozen blueberries
- 2 packages powdered fruit pectin
- ¾ cup lemon juice
- 12 cups sugar

Directions::
mix lemon juice and berries and slightly crush.
Pour in a pan, stir in pectin and boil over high heat for 10 minutes, ensuring you stir constantly.
Add sugar and leave to boil for 1 minute and continue stirring.
Remove from the heat and scoop off any foam.
Ladle mixture into hot jars, ensuring you leave ¼-inch headspace.
Scoop bubbles and adjust the lids.
In a boiling water canner, process the mixture for 10 minutes.
Leave to cool and enjoy.
Nutrition Calories: 98 kcal Fat: 0 g Cholesterol: 0 mg Sodium: 0 mg
Carbohydrate: 25 g Fiber: 0 g Protein: 0 g

Blueberry Vanilla Jam

Preparation time: 10 minutes
Cooking time: 10 minutes
Canning time: 8 minutes
Servings: 2 ½-pint jars
Ingredients:
- ½ cups blueberries
- 1 tsp calcium water
- 1 cup granulated sugar
- 1 tsp Pomona's pectin
- 3 tbsp lemon juice
- ½ tsp vanilla bean paste

Directions::
Pour water into a large pot and heat over medium heat.
Submerge a clean jar in a water bath and leave it to boil.
Evenly mix pectin and sugar in a bowl.
Mash berries until you have 2 cups and leave out a few whole berries.
Pour into a saucepan and add calcium water and lemon juice.
Add vanilla bean paste to the saucepan, boil, and keep stirring.
Whip pectin and sugar mixture until it dissolves.
Stir until it boils.
Remove from heat, add vanilla paste and keep stirring.
Put jam in a jar and tighten lids and leave ¼-inch.
Process it in a boiling water bath.
After 8 minutes, remove it from the water and leave it for 24 hours to cool.
Refrigerate.
Nutrition Calories per 2 tbsp: 45 kcal Protein: 0 g Carbohydrates: 11 g Fat: 0 g Sodium: 0 mg

Balsamic Tomato Jam

Preparation time: 10 minutes
Cooking time: 30 minutes
Servings: 2 pints
Ingredients:
- 2 lb tomatoes, diced
- 1 tsp kosher salt
- ½ cup rosemary, freshly chopped
- 2 tbsp brown sugar
- 2 tsp freshly ground black pepper
- ¼ cup balsamic vinegar

Directions::
Add tomatoes to a medium-size pot and cook over medium-low heat for 10 minutes.
Once tomatoes start releasing the liquid, Add remaining ingredients and lower the heat to low.
Continue cooking for 20 minutes, or until the mixture reaches ajam-like consistency.
Pour into 4 ½-pint jars and seal tightly.
Refrigerate.
Nutrition Calories per 2 tbsp: 20 kcal Protein: 0.4 g Carbohydrates: 4 g Fat: 0 g Sodium: 83 mg

CONCLUSION

After reading all of this you might be feeling a little overwhelmed. Don't panic, this is natural. Do not let a large amount of information phase you. This book was not written to scare you or make you feel incompetent. No. If anything, this book was written to help you navigate through the challenges home canning may throw in your direction.

Canning your own food is a deeply satisfying activity. When you take a look at your canned foods and you realize that you were able to do it on your own, it will fuel the motivation you need to turn this into a regular habit. If you choose to can your own food on a regular basis, you will notice a decline in the amount of money you use to buy produce and other canned foods. Home canning will also influence your eating habits in a positive way. The foods you will be preserved will be far healthier than the preserved foods that are sold in supermarkets.

Once you get the hang of canning your own food, you will be unstoppable! I will not lie to you and tell you that everything will be easy – especially the first couple of times. You will make a couple of mistakes and you might make a mess of your kitchen too. This is expected – you are a beginner after all .
As time goes by, though, the number of mistakes you make will decrease, and eventually, you won't need this guide to assist you. You will be able to come up with creative recipes of your own! This all has to start with the first steps, the first steps being you are giving this a chance.

If you aren't feeling confident in your abilities, try out the easiest water bath canning recipe in this book. You can also find a number of safe and USDA approved recipes online. There are a number of forums dedicated to offering support to home canning beginners. Don't let your fears stop you from trying out this great method of preserving your own food. It is a highly rewarding experience that is capable of benefitting you for years to come.

You won't regret trying it out.

Thank you again for downloading this book!
I hope this book was able to help you know the basics of food canning and preservation. I hope that this book was able to clearly explain the different concepts and rules when it comes to canning and preserving food. I also hope that you'll be able to follow all the instructions indicated in this book.

The next step is to apply all the things that you have learned from this book. Remember that knowledge without application is useless. Look for canning and preservation recipes online or from different books and start doing them yourself. Just see to it that you will always take into consideration the reminders, especially the fact that you first have to understand the method that you are going to carry out before you start doing anything.

Thank you and good luck!

www.ingramcontent.com/pod-product-compliance
Lightning Source LLC
Chambersburg PA
CBHW050412120526
44590CB00015B/1935